Contents

New Directions for
Higher Education

Betsy O. Barefoot
Jillian L. Kinzie
Co-editors

WITHDRAWAL

In Search of Self: Exploring Student Identity Development

Chad Hanson

EDITOR

Number 166 • Summer 2014
Jossey-Bass
San Francisco

IN SEARCH OF SELF: EXPLORING STUDENT IDENTITY DEVELOPMENT
Chad Hanson
New Directions for Higher Education, no. 166
Betsy O. Barefoot and Jillian L. Kinzie, Co-editors

Microfilm copies of issues and articles are available in 16mm and 35mm, as well as microfiche in 105mm, through University Microfilms Inc., 300 North Zeeb Road, Ann Arbor, MI 48106-1346.

NEW DIRECTIONS FOR HIGHER EDUCATION (ISSN 0271-0560, electronic ISSN 1536-0741) is part of The Jossey-Bass Higher and Adult Education Series and is published quarterly by Wiley Subscription Services, Inc., A Wiley Company, at Jossey-Bass, One Montgomery Street, Suite 1200, San Francisco, CA 94104-4594. Periodicals Postage Paid at San Francisco, California, and at additional mailing offices. POSTMASTER: Send address changes to New Directions for Higher Education, Jossey-Bass, One Montgomery Street, Suite 1200, San Francisco, CA 94104-4594.

New Directions for Higher Education is indexed in Current Index to Journals in Education (ERIC); Higher Education Abstracts.

Individual subscription rate (in USD): $89 per year US/Can/Mex, $113 rest of world; institutional subscription rate: $311 US, $351 Can/Mex, $385 rest of world. Single copy rate: $29. Electronic only–all regions: $89 individual, $311 institutional; Print & Electronic–US: $98 individual, $357 institutional; Print & Electronic–Canada/Mexico: $98 individual, $397 institutional; Print & Electronic–Rest of World: $122 individual, $431 institutional.

Editorial correspondence should be sent to the Co-editor, Betsy O. Barefoot, Gardner Institute, Box 72, Brevard, NC 28712.

Cover photograph © Digital Vision

www.josseybass.com

Editor's Notes

All over the country, in the months of May and June, colleges conduct graduation ceremonies. At the end of the ritual, students move their tassels from one side of their mortarboard to the other. They toss their caps into the air. Then they rush to meet their relatives, as new and different people. In *We're Losing Our Minds*, Richard Hersh and Richard Keeling (2011) claim, "At its root, the idea of higher learning is one of positive change: the student who graduates will not be, and should not be, the same person as the one who started college" (p. 6). During a college education, we develop a new sense of who we are. The term "graduate" becomes a part of our identities.

In some ways, we all acknowledge the transformative purpose of attending a college or university. In the past 20 years, however, under pressure to document learning, many of us adopted the perspective and methods of 1950s behaviorism. We grew attached to the framework popularized by John B. Watson (1913) and B. F. Skinner (1964) in the early and middle parts of the 20th century. We often see teaching as a stimulus and learning as a response. Short-term, observable outcomes became the currency that we value. But even B. F. Skinner knew the limits of his views when applied to education. In an essay for the *New Scientist*, he wrote, "Education is what survives when what has been learned has been forgotten" (Skinner, 1964, p. 484). The development of skills and the acquisition of knowledge are important, but they are not the most crucial or lasting components of the college experience. Higher education, at its best, changes the lives of graduates. Thus, in *The American College*, Nevitt Sanford (1962) suggested, "The proper study of the effects of college ... is the study of lives" (p. 809). In spite of such advice, we often feel compelled to assess short-term, cognitive outcomes.

As an example, the American Sociological Association, the largest organization in my field, recently renamed its Section on Undergraduate Education. The group is now called the Section on Teaching and Learning. For those unfamiliar with the discipline of sociology, allow me to explain. When sociologists willingly shrink their research on a social institution down to one single pair of variables, something profound has taken place: a reduction in the scope of our work, a disregard for tradition, and from my perspective, a change for the worse. Sociologists formerly viewed education as a rich, complex, and meaningful process. For instance, it was a team of sociologists, led by Howard Becker, who suggested of medical education, "Science and skill do not make a physician; one must also be initiated into the status of physician; to be accepted one must have learned to play the part of a physician in the drama of medicine" (Becker, Geer, Hughes, & Strauss, 1961, p. 4).

In the past, sociologists attempted to understand the social roles, institutional norms, and cultural values at work in the production of life in schools. Today, in sociology and other fields, we tend to forgo our own perspectives and take up cognitive or behaviorist psychology when we turn our attention to students. The intent of this volume is to give a voice to scholars who use a range of means to conceive and study the process of becoming a college or university graduate.

Scope and Purpose

In what follows, educators and researchers in a variety of fields offer their views on how we might improve our efforts to understand the impact of higher education. In contrast to the current emphasis on psychometrics, the authors of the following chapters suggest methods that allow for a consideration of the personal changes that occur as students make progress toward the goal of becoming educated. Each contributor offers faculty, staff, and those who work in student development the means by which to explore how a college education affords students a chance to develop a new set of traits and characteristics.

Between the covers of this volume, you will find the perspectives and methods of sociologists, psychologists, an anthropologist, a political scientist, an occupational therapist, a community organizer, and higher education specialists. From their different disciplines, each contributor moves us in the direction of understanding the broad and long-ranging effects of becoming a college graduate.

Chapter Outline

In Chapter 1, I describe the cultural context that gives shape to our efforts when it comes to assessing students. I discuss the historical forces that moved staff and faculty members to focus narrowly on cognitive outcomes. I conclude by suggesting that the focus on learning has kept us from undertaking a broader assessment of the college experience.

In Chapter 2, Dan P. McAdams and Jennifer Guo raise a question that students ought to have an occasion to address, namely, "How Shall I Live?" McAdams and Guo offer the steps to conducting a narrative interview as a way to allow students to reflect upon the nature of the time they spend in college. They suggest that we should create a way for students to reflect upon the process of developing a meaningful life story. McAdams serves as director of the Foley Center for the Study of Lives, an organization that provides resources to those interested in the measures that individuals use to craft life stories out of their experience.

Marcia B. Baxter Magolda is well known to those who work in student affairs and those who study student development. In Chapter 3, Baxter Magolda describes the concept of self-authorship, an idea that she developed in a series of publications including *Making Their Own Way: Narratives for Transforming Higher Education to Promote Self-Development* (Baxter Magolda, 2004). In the course of self-authorship, students come to take command of their thought processes and ultimately their futures as employees, citizens, and members of families. In this chapter, Baxter Magolda suggests the formation of learning partnerships as a method for leading students to the stage where they can engage in self-authorship.

Many scholars have pointed out how the field of sociology has been underutilized in the study of postsecondary schools (Hanson, 2005). In Chapter 4, Peter Kaufman outlines the basic tenets of symbolic interactionism, the framework that often informs sociologists' studies of self and identity. Kaufman (2003) draws on years of prior research to suggest that symbolic interaction holds the potential to help educators and college leaders to understand the process that students move through as they work to build self-concepts that reflect their status as newly educated members of society.

Twenty-five years ago, John C. Weidman (1989) suggested that colleges and universities function as socializing agents. In addition to improving skills, Weidman encouraged scholars and practitioners to give thought to the way our schools shape students' values and aspirations. In Chapter 5, Weidman, Linda DeAngelo, and Kathryn A. Bethea review a series of recent studies that lend support to the idea that our schools serve as socializing institutions. Afterward, they recommend a path for the continued analysis of the extent to which education socializes students.

Colleges rarely take steps to assess the question of whether they produce vigorous citizens, but preparation for citizenship is one of the most frequently cited elements of institutional mission statements. In Chapter 6, Katy J. Harriger shares findings from a project that established a group of undergraduate Democracy Fellows at Wake Forest University. Harriger describes the democratic dispositions that resulted from the project. Her findings suggest possibilities for programs that could encourage the formation of civic identities.

When we think about the broad and long-term goals of schooling, we often think of the liberal arts or general education. In Chapter 7, Steve Hoppes turns our attention to preprofessional training. In this chapter, Hoppes describes his use of the technique known as autoethnography. The method was pioneered as a means to describe the relationship between individuals and their environment. Hoppes and his colleagues at the University of Oklahoma have made use of the technique as a way for occupational therapy students to document the changes they go through as they prepare themselves for lives as new professionals (Hoppes, 2005). Hoppes uses a case study to give readers a sense of the potential for autoethnography as a teaching tool and as a method for recording identity development.

Cathy A. Small conducted one of the most well-respected and widely read contemporary ethnographies of university life, *My Freshman Year* (Nathan, 2005). Her work as an anthropologist of higher education led to the conclusion that the experience that students have outside the classroom can impact them more than the act of going to class or writing papers or taking examinations. She used that insight to structure a course that purposefully combined American and international students, with the hope that an encounter with the "other" would give participants an opportunity to rethink the traits that make them who they are. In Chapter 8, she offers results from an analysis of the course. She concludes with suggestions for future research and applications.

In Chapter 9, David G. Blumenkrantz and Marc B. Goldstein expand upon the idea that the field of anthropology may help us understand the ritual of attending and graduating from a postsecondary institution. They begin by explaining how the college experience serves as a rite of passage, whether we conceive it that way or not. They raise a series of questions that college personnel can use to help create a positive environment for incoming freshmen. Then they conclude by explaining how the postsecondary ritual holds the potential to become an intentional way for students to come of age in our culture.

In Chapter 10, Robert J. Nash and Jennifer J. J. Jang provide us with a reminder that education is a meaningful part of a person's life. They offer the core components of a meaning-making pedagogy that Nash developed over the course of a career that spans four decades and includes a series of publications, such as *Helping College Students Find Purpose* (Nash & Murray, 2010). In this final chapter, Nash and Jang raise questions that are suitable to ask in a variety of disciplines and settings—anywhere students make the transition from newly matriculated enrollees to graduates.

Conclusion

Here in the 21st century, we have a propensity to think of colleges and universities as Skinner Boxes. Too often, we shrink our thoughts on these large, complicated institutions down to the level of teaching and learning: a stimulus and a response. This volume offers scholars, educators, and administrators a host of ways to acknowledge and explore the rich, diverse, and meaningful experience of becoming educated. Each chapter is worth thoughtful consideration. Throughout this volume, you will find the techniques and rationale for studying the process that students move through as they grapple to form new versions of themselves. The authors present and discuss teaching techniques, research methods, and organizational approaches. Each chapter provides a unique means of understanding the nature of the college experience and its role in student development.

Chad Hanson
Editor

References

Baxter Magolda, M. B. (2004). *Making their own way: Narratives for transforming higher education to promote self-development*. Sterling, VA: Stylus Publishing.

Becker, H., Geer, B., Hughes, E., & Strauss, A. (1961). *The boys in white: Student culture in medical school*. Chicago, IL: University of Chicago Press.

Hanson, C. (2005). The scholarship of teaching and learning—done by sociologists: Let's make that the sociology of higher education. *Teaching Sociology, 33*(4), 411–416.

Hersh, R., & Keeling, R. (2011). *We're losing our minds: Rethinking higher education*. New York, NY: Palgrave Macmillan.

Hoppes, S. (2005). When a child dies the world should stop spinning: An autoethnography exploring the impact of family loss on occupation. *American Journal of Occupational Therapy, 59*(1), 78–87.

Kaufman, P. (2003). Learning to not labor: How working-class individuals construct middle-class identities. *The Sociological Quarterly, 44*(3), 481–504.

Nash, R., & Murray, M. (2010). *Helping college students find purpose: The campus guide to meaning-making*. San Francisco, CA: Jossey-Bass.

Nathan, R. [C. A. Small]. (2005). *My freshman year: What a professor learned by becoming a student*. Ithaca, NY: Cornell University Press.

Sanford, N. (1962). *The American college*. New York, NY: Wiley.

Skinner, B. F. (1964). New methods and new aims in teaching. *New Scientist, 122*(5), 483–484.

Watson, J. B. (1913). Psychology as the behaviorist views it. *Psychological Review, 20*, 158–177.

Weidman, J. C. (1989). Undergraduate socialization: A conceptual approach. In J. C. Smart (Ed.), *Higher education: Handbook of theory and research* (Vol. 5, pp. 289–322). New York, NY: Agathon Press.

CHAD HANSON serves as the chairman of the Department of Sociology and Social Work at Casper College.

1

In the past 20 years, scholars and practitioners have committed to measuring the cognitive outcomes of education. In this chapter, the author assesses the movement that focuses on cognition, to the exclusion of other outcomes. An identity-based framework is offered as an alternative.

Changing How We Think About the Goals of Higher Education

Chad Hanson

Howard Bowen (1977) once wrote, "The impact of higher education is likely to be determined more by the kind of people college graduates become than by what they know when they leave college" (p. 270). It is easy to see the truth in such a statement. Even so, in the past two decades many of us turned our attention to documenting one aspect of change in college: cognitive development. As professionals, we became committed to measuring the skills and knowledge that people learn in courses and degree programs. For a range of reasons that include culture, politics, and accreditation, we made learning outcomes, rather than identity development, the centerpiece of our effort to understand how colleges affect students.

In what follows, I offer an analysis of the historical shift that made the assessment of learning outcomes a priority. I consider the social forces that moved our attention away from identity development and toward short-term cognitive outcomes. In the process, I hope to demonstrate why the authors in this volume offer a much-needed alternative to the common psychometrics that we use to measure the outcomes of the college experience.

A Culture Shift

In the beginning, American higher education was patterned primarily after the colleges of the United Kingdom. Our schools reflected conventions carried to North America from the campuses of Oxford and Cambridge. Our institutions saw character formation as central to their mission. Then, in the first two decades of the 20th century, the purpose of our schools started to change. We began to move away from the British archetype. We became

New Directions for Higher Education, no. 166, Summer 2014 © 2014 Wiley Periodicals, Inc.
Published online in Wiley Online Library (wileyonlinelibrary.com) • DOI: 10.1002/he.20090

invested in the German model, emphasizing research and the production of knowledge (Rudolph & Thelin, 1990).

By 1968, when Christopher Jencks and David Reisman published *The Academic Revolution*, the shift from "teaching college" to "research university" had unfolded. The move in the direction of research served to privilege science- and technology-oriented fields. Experimental methods became a desirable, and lucrative, alternative to the arts and letters (Wilson, 2013). The study of how college affects students came of age in this period, and the perspectives and methods of hard science grew dominant. To this day, the distinction between "hard" and "soft" reveals our preference. Over time, the field of cognitive psychology became aligned with the methods of natural science. Thus, it was poised to become the "hard" face of our efforts to understand student development. Psychometrics became our benchmarks, and we abandoned the big questions about who our students become.

In *The Learning Self: Understanding the Potential for Transformation*, Mark Tennant (2012) explains how our affinity for the hard or natural sciences made it unlikely for faculty or staff to study student identity development. He wrote:

> The self is not a natural entity that can be objectively studied. It has a historical rather than a natural status. That is, unlike objects in the physical world, the self is not something that is independent of the way we think, theorize, and talk about it. (p. 5)

Identities are created as we think, talk, and tell stories about who we are, where we have been, and what we have done. Any thorough study of how people change in college would seem to require an analysis of the narratives that students use to develop identities—a sense of what they were like before they started and who they became during the course of their education.

When graduates reflect on what their schooling meant to them, they put their narrative interpretations on display. Consider the following quote from the novelist Andre Dubus. In his memoirs, he wrote: " … all that booklearning had seemed to open doors inside me that led to a higher part of myself, one that was more evolved and thoughtful, reasonable and idealistic … " (Dubus, 2011, p. 198). Technical skills and bits of knowledge seem trivial beside such a statement. Dubus illustrates the value of asking students to describe the kinds of people they are becoming. But the answers to such questions are not what we consider objective.

The stories that students use to make sense of who they are do not fit into charts or graphs. They clash with the culture of positivism that we maintain in the academy. Many scholars feel bound to use the methods of science as opposed to those of the humanities. We see stories as "soft," and thus we find one reason why faculty rarely assess the meaning of the college experience. Administrators and policy makers have also paid scant attention to the web of narrative that students inhabit.

The Politics of Studying Students

In 1973, Burton Clark published a prescient article, "Development of the Sociology of Higher Education." In this work, Clark suggested that studies of schools are influenced by politics. He cited the tendency for research agendas to become "voiced around the immediate needs of administration and public policy" (p. 10), as opposed to the perspectives of scholars or the demands of the subject. With respect to policy, research questions become voiced around the concerns of partisan authors and elected officials.

In his books and articles, Stanley Fish resists easy classification as a member of the political left or right. Still, in his most well-known treatise on faculty, *Save the World on Your Own Time* (Fish, 2008), he takes a conservative position on the purpose of education. Fish urges a narrow role for colleges and universities. He offers faculty a simple set of instructions: "teach materials and confer skills" (p. 176). He claims that by limiting our efforts to nurturing certain abilities, we protect ourselves from the accusation that "we venture into precincts (of politics, morality, and ethics) not properly ours" (p. 176). Conservative tomes, such as Allan Bloom's (1987) *The Closing of the American Mind: How Higher Education Has Failed Democracy and Impoverished the Souls of Today's Students* and E. D. Hirsch's (1987) *Cultural Literacy: What Every American Needs to Know*, mirror Fish's line of thought. For conservative commentators, the aim of schooling is to ensure that graduates possess a proper stock of knowledge. Questions about whom our students become fall outside of this agenda.

Liberal-minded leaders are motivated by different forces. Generations of Democrats have concerned themselves with improving access to higher education (Bailey & Smith-Morest, 2006). Liberals believe that it is the role of public institutions to address issues of inequality. Thus, they see education as a way to aid those who suffer from disadvantages. Concern for the underprivileged has led to a line of research on the self and identity, but the studies are often limited in scope. Subjects are chosen on the basis of their membership in a group identified as a minority—for example: women, people of color, or gay and lesbian students (Evans, Forney, Guido, Patton, & Renn, 2010).

Studying the identities of those from diverse backgrounds is important work. Efforts to document the cognitive outcomes of education are necessary, too. Taken together, however, the emphasis on documenting particular skills, and the focus on the race, gender, and sexuality of students have made it unlikely for scholars to build a program of research aimed at understanding identity development—writ large. The political climate steers us toward diversity studies on one hand (Jacoby, 1999) and documenting cognitive outcomes on the other (Arum & Roksa, 2011).

Some might argue that as ivory towers, institutions of higher learning are insulated from politics. To some degree, colleges and universities enjoy autonomy, but the autonomy is not complete. Through the accreditation process, institutions are held to politically acceptable standards. For the past 12 years, I have served as a consultant-evaluator for the nation's largest regional accrediting agency, the Higher Learning Commission of the North Central Association of Colleges and Schools. During that time, I have worked as a member of teams dispatched to assess institutions from Ohio to Arizona. Teams differ with respect to their priorities, but on two measures I find consistency. First, we expect schools to assess cognitive learning. Second, we make sure that institutions commit to assuring diversity within their staff, students, and faculty.

Even when a college's mission statement suggests that the institution exists to create certain kinds of people—good citizens, for example—I am not aware of a case where an accrediting agency required an institution to assess the question of whether their graduates become vigorous citizens. I make this point not to underscore the shortcomings of the accreditation process, but rather to illustrate how political preferences shape our inquiries.

The Rise of Human Capital Development

There is one aspect of higher education that politicians agree upon. Across the spectrum, postsecondary schools are seen as engines of economic development (Engell & Dangerfield, 2005). Education is thought of as career preparation, and when we conceive education as training for the labor force, the effect has been that we become less interested in broader questions about the traits or character of graduates. Instead, we see students, narrowly, as economic resources. We see them as skill sets, capable of adding value to an organization (Barnett, 1994). We focus on producing outcomes and abilities. Then we think of our graduates as *products* that we market to employers. But in fact, the experience of attending a college or university is a *process* through which students grow into and become educated people (Chickering, 1969).

When we think of students as a human form of capital, the view potentially restricts our intellectual terrain. We run the risk of limiting ourselves to questions about what students know or how they perform prescribed tasks. We lose sight of the notion that schools allow people to forge new selves. During the process of higher education, students are "actively experimenting with and consolidating a sense of identity: who they are, what they can do well, what is important to them, how they want others to see them, and so forth" (King & Kitchener, 1994, p. 203). Whether students are of traditional age and establishing independence or nontraditional and in the process of changing their identity, education offers individuals a chance to renew what it means to be themselves.

The human self or identity is a collection of memories (McCall & Simmons, 1966). For graduates, a college is an alma mater, a set of experiences, and a bundle of recollections. The experience of college becomes part of a student's life story and a part of their past. The past has a profound influence upon whom we become and how we act. Our personal histories "take us to places that counsel and instruct, by showing us who we are and by showing us where we have been" (Chapman, 1979, p. 46). Those places and stories confer social status and they order behaviors, often, for the remainder of a person's days. The most important feature of a college education is the process or experience of becoming educated.

Those who take a human capital approach to students do so, in large part, because they believe employers see graduates as economic entities. New research from the Association of American Colleges and Universities (AAC&U, 2013) suggests that businesses see employees as more than walking skill sets or indexes of knowledge, however. It turns out that when employers add to their workforce, they seek certain kinds of people. In the AAC&U (2013) study entitled *It Takes More Than a Major: Employer Priorities for College Learning and Student Success*, 318 executives in the private and not-for-profit sectors were asked to describe what they look for when they seek to fill new positions. The study suggests that employers place the highest priority on finding people with "integrity" and people who are willing to make "ethical judgments." Organizations also seek employees with an interest in "continued new learning." They hire people who "give back to the communities" they are from, and they look for those who are "comfortable working with colleagues, and/or clients from diverse cultural backgrounds" (p. 7).

Knowledge and skills are not necessarily the most important factors when it comes to the question of whom a business will hire. Picture a typical job interview. Employers rarely conduct knowledge or skills tests as part of the hiring process. An interview is an exercise in storytelling. Candidates are asked to tell the story of themselves: who they are, what they are like, where they have been, and what their futures hold in store.

I do not see college students as human capital. In my mind human beings and capital are two very different things. Even if you are comfortable thinking of people as economic units, however, the evidence suggests the best thing we can do for employers is to provide them with a selection of ethical, open-hearted, and intellectually curious people (AAC&U, 2013).

Conclusion

During a brief period in the 1970s, the study of student identity enjoyed some level of prestige. Today, however, books like Arthur Chickering's (1969) *Education and Identity* stand on shelves as reminders of a time when it looked like our institutions might conduct wide-ranging investigations into the question of how our students change in college. Alas, for reasons that relate to politics, positivism, and questionable assumptions about what is best for the economy, the focus on identity diminished. At the risk of sounding obvious, these are not fair reasons to avoid the study of how education becomes a part of our life stories.

The cognitive outcomes of education will likely remain the subject of our attention, at least in the short term. I am aware that we are not going to stop producing charts and graphs. But at this point, we would also do well to acknowledge that the experience of schooling holds the potential to serve as a life-changing milepost. Test scores and rubrics contribute little to the process of constructing a personal, civic, or professional identity. Students use narratives to build and maintain a sense of who they are. Schools hold the promise of helping students to develop wiser, more thoughtful, and idealistic versions of themselves. Our students deserve an educational experience intended to ensure that the memories will last and guide them into the future. In the months and years ahead, let us not forget, when it is at its best, higher education is a meaningful, memorable, and formative process.

References

Arum, A., & Roksa, J. (2011). *Academically adrift: Limited learning on college campuses.* Chicago, IL: University of Chicago Press.

Association of American Colleges and Universities (AAC&U). (2013). *It takes more than a major: Employer priorities for college learning and student success.* Washington, DC: Author.

Bailey, T., & Smith-Morest, V. (Eds.). (2006). *Defending the community college equity agenda.* Baltimore, MD: Johns Hopkins University Press.

Barnett, R. (1994). *The limits of competence: Knowledge, higher education, and society.* Buckingham, England: The Society for Research into Higher Education & Open University Press.

Bloom, A. (1987). *The closing of the American mind: How higher education has failed democracy and impoverished the souls of today's students.* New York, NY: Simon and Schuster.

Bowen, H. (1977). *Investment in learning: The individual and social value of higher education.* San Francisco, CA: Jossey-Bass.

Chapman, W. (1979). *Preserving the past.* London, England: Dent.

Chickering, A. (1969). *Education and identity.* San Francisco, CA: Jossey-Bass.

Clark, B. (1973). Development of the sociology of higher education. *Sociology of Education, 46*(4), 2–14.

Dubus, A., III. (2011). *Townie: A memoir.* New York, NY: W.W. Norton & Company.

Engell, J., & Dangerfield, A. (2005). *Saving higher education in the age of money.* Charlottesville: University of Virginia Press.

Evans, N., Forney, D., Guido, F., Patton, L., & Renn, K. (Eds.). (2010). *Student development in college: Theory, research, and practice* (2nd ed.). San Francisco, CA: Jossey-Bass.

Fish, S. (2008). *Save the world on your own time.* New York, NY: Oxford University Press.

Hirsch, E. D. (1987). *Cultural literacy: What every American needs to know.* New York, NY: Houghton Mifflin.

Jacoby, R. (1999). *The end of utopia: Politics and culture in an age of apathy.* New York, NY: Basic Books.

Jencks, C., & Reisman, D. (1968). *The academic revolution*. New York, NY: Doubleday.

King, P., & Kitchener, K. (1994). *Developing reflective judgment*. San Francisco, CA: Jossey-Bass.

McCall, G., & Simmons, J. (1966). *Identities and interactions*. New York, NY: The Free Press.

Rudolph, F., & Thelin, J. (1990). *The American college and university: A history*. Athens: University of Georgia Press.

Tennant, M. (2012). *The learning self: Understanding the potential for transformation*. San Francisco, CA: Jossey-Bass.

Wilson, R. (2013, July 15). Humanities scholars see declining prestige, not a lack of interest. *The Chronicle of Higher Education*, 59(42), A8–A9.

CHAD HANSON serves as the chairman of the Department of Sociology and Social Work at Casper College.

2

This chapter applies the concept of narrative identity to college student development. The authors describe a narrative interview method that can be used to promote the development of a purposeful life story in the college years.

How Shall I Live? Constructing a Life Story in the College Years

Dan P. McAdams, Jennifer Guo

American educators and the lay public have long considered the college years to be a time when young people struggle to find out who they are and how they will lead lives that matter. In a lecture he regularly gave to Harvard College students in the 1890s, William James posed the question: "What Makes a Life Significant?" After considering different options, James argued that human *ideals* confer deep meaning and significance on a life, and college should be designed to promote the exploration of ideals: "Education, enlarging as it does our horizon and perspective, is a means of multiplying our ideals, of bringing new ones into view" (Schwehn & Bass, 2006, p. 25). The great psychoanalytic theorist Erik Erikson (1950) developed the same theme in asserting that the search for *identity* constitutes the major psychosocial challenge for adolescents and young adults. As Erikson saw it, identity encompasses, among other things, the religious, political, and ethical beliefs and values that a person ultimately embraces (ideals) and the occupational or productive roles that a person will pursue as he or she moves into adulthood (work). The college years are prime time, Erikson believed, for exploring different options with regard to ideals and work and eventually committing to particular ideological positions and work roles that promise to provide a life with some degree of significance, meaning, and purpose.

At coffee shops and campus events, in residence halls, at the gym, over the Internet, and almost everywhere else, college students share their thoughts and feelings about their ideals, their work, and their identities with

Preparation of this chapter was supported by a grant to the first author from the Foley Family Foundation to establish the Foley Center for the Study of Lives at Northwestern University.

New Directions for Higher Education, no. 166, Summer 2014 © 2014 Wiley Periodicals, Inc.
Published online in Wiley Online Library (wileyonlinelibrary.com) • DOI: 10.1002/he.20091

each other and with parents, counselors, student affairs professionals, and anybody else they feel they can trust. For many young people, college may be the ideal forum for "self talk," for exploring the self and learning about others through conversation. A wide range of theories and research findings in psychology suggest that conversations about personal experiences contribute greatly to the formation of identity in adolescence and young adulthood (McLean, Pasupathi, & Pals, 2007).

In this chapter, we describe a set of ideas and tools for promoting identity explorations that capitalize on the tendency of young people to talk, sometimes incessantly, about themselves. The key concept is *narrative identity*, which may be defined as a person's internalized and evolving story of the self (McAdams & McLean, 2013). The tools to be proposed derive from interview-based research into narrative identity, and much of this research has been conducted with midlife adults (McAdams, 2013). We believe that our research approach may be repurposed as a model for identity development exercises in college to be used by educators, counselors, and other college professionals who work directly with students. We believe our approach holds promise for its ability to provide students with a framework for organizing their conversations about themselves in ways that facilitate the development of the animating ideals and purpose-giving roles that lie at the heart of identity.

Narrative Identity: The Construction of a Life Story

Erikson (1950) believed that identity functions to provide a person's life with a deep sense of temporal continuity. When individuals have formulated a coherent identity, they not only know who they are but they also understand how they came to be and where their lives may be headed in the future. Identity works to integrate the reconstructed past and imagined future into a psychosocial pattern that makes sense to the self and to the people and the institutions who bear witness to the self's development. Over the past 20 years, a growing number of researchers in personality, developmental, cognitive, and cultural psychology have argued that identity manages to affirm temporal continuity through a person's construction of a life story. As people make sense of their lives through narrative, they come to articulate an understanding of how their past relates to the present and the imagined future; they develop a story about how they came to be the person they are becoming (Bruner, 1990; McAdams, 1985). Narrative identity *is* that story—an evolving and internalized narrative of the self that begins to take form in adolescence.

Although researchers examine narrative identity in many different ways, a standard research approach for delineating the content and the structure of a person's life story is to engage the research participant in a structured Life Story Interview (McAdams, 1985, 2013). As outlined in Table 2.1, the interviewer asks a series of questions designed to uncover

Table 2.1. Outline of a Standard Life Story Interview

Life Chapters	Think of your life as if it were a book—a novel with chapters. What would the chapters be? Divide your life story into its main chapters, and for each chapter provide a title and brief plot summary. Explain what marks the end of one chapter and the beginning of the next.

Key Scenes
  High Point
  Low Point
  Turning Point
  Positive Childhood Scene
  Negative Childhood Scene
  Vivid Adolescent Scene
  Vivid Adult Scene
  One Other Important
  Scene
	Focus on a few specific moments or episodes that stand out as being especially memorable or important in your life story. For each scene, describe in detail what happened, who was there, what you were thinking and feeling in the scene, and what significance you believe the scene has in the context of your entire life story. Why do you think you chose this scene? What might the scene say about who you were or are?

Life Challenge	Identify the most important challenge, struggle, or conflict you have faced in your life. Describe what the challenge is, how it came to be, and how you have tried to address it or cope with it.
Future Script	What does the next chapter of your life story look like? Describe where you think your life is headed in the future. What are your main goals for the future? How do you plan to achieve those goals?

Ideological Setting
  Religious
  Political
  Most Important Value
	Consider here your most important beliefs and values about life and the world. First, describe any religious and/or ethical values and beliefs that you consider to be important for your life. How did you develop those values and beliefs? Next, consider beliefs and values that apply to politics and/or social relationships. Describe those values and beliefs and how you came to hold them. Finally, what do you consider to be the most important value in life? Why?

Life Theme	Thinking back over what you have said in this interview, do you see a theme or motif that runs through the story of your life? What might it be?

Note: Variations on this general interview format have been developed for many different kinds of studies, each tailored to the aims of the study. For more information on different versions and formats of the life story interview go to http://www.sesp.northwestern.edu/foley/.

key scenes, characters, trends, and themes in the person's life story. Typically, the narrator begins by dividing his or her life into "chapters" and providing a brief plot summary for each. Next, the interviewer asks the narrator to focus on a few key events that stand out as especially memorable or important in the life story. These typically include a life-story "high point" (the greatest or happiest moment in the story), "low point" (the worst or unhappiest moment in the story), "turning point" (a moment of significant change or transition in the story), and a series of other scenes that are notable for their emotional/psychological quality or timing in the life course. For each scene, narrators describe what happened in the moment, what they were thinking and feeling, how the scene was ultimately resolved, and what they see as a central lesson or insight about the self that might be derived from the scene.

Narrative identity is nearly as much about the imagined future as it is about the reconstructed past. Therefore, the interviewer next asks the narrator to imagine what is in store for the future and to describe what the next chapter in the life story might be, along with dreams, plans, goals, and fears regarding the future. The narrator then elaborates upon the fundamental beliefs, values, and attitudes that situate the story within an ideological setting (McAdams, 1985). These include beliefs and values that typically speak to religious, ethical, and political–social issues. Finally, the narrator is asked to reflect upon the narrative as a whole and identify a central theme or motif that seems to run through the story.

In considering how research on narrative identity might be repurposed as an intervention to be used by college professionals, we follow the lead of Schwehn and Bass (2006) who delineate three different "vocabularies" that "people use today in their efforts to think and talk about the kind of life that they most admire and would therefore most like to lead" (p. 40). These are the vocabularies of *authenticity*, *virtue*, and *vocation*. Our experience with life stories suggests that each of the three vocabularies regularly finds its way into the narrative identities that American adults construct to make sense of their lives. Each provides a language for describing a worthy life—a life of significance and deep meaning.

Authenticity: Finding My Real Story.   To be authentic is to present and express the self *as it really is*. People feel authentic when they sense that they are cutting through the pretenses of everyday social conventions and expressing something "true" and "real." They know who they are, and they express themselves accordingly, even when such expressions defy societal norms and expectations. Going back at least as far as Ralph Waldo Emerson's (1841/1993) *Self-Reliance*, Americans have tended to value the authenticity of the individual over and against what are sometimes seen as artificial, and even oppressive, strictures of the group (McAdams, 2013; Taylor, 1991). Be true to yourself, we are told. Don't follow the crowd.

Research participants in studies of narrative identity tend to construe the Life Story Interview as an opportunity to tell their own unique story. Simply going through the interview process, then, can itself constitute an exercise in personal authenticity. As the participants see it, the interviewer wants to know what *really* happened in their own lives and what they—the participants—*truly* believe the meaning of the events to be. Accordingly, research participants often use a language of authenticity in describing chapters, scenes, and future prospects in their lives. They will say that a particular decision they made "shows who I truly am" or "illustrates something that has always been true for me." They will talk about how they pursued a particular goal or relationship because "I really wanted that" or because it summoned forth deeply felt emotions of joy, excitement, love, or wonder— feeling states that they associate with authentic experience.

In that many college students struggle to determine who they really are and what they truly want to do with their lives, the Life Story Interview can serve to promote self-exploration by encouraging students to engage explicitly in the discourse of personal authenticity. The interview format works in a nonthreatening way. Rather than putting the student on the spot by posing threatening questions about the future, the interview focuses a great deal of attention on the past, gently urging the student to explore what past experiences might indicate about the particular kind of person they have become and are becoming. Because the interview implicitly places a premium on personal authenticity, it can provide practice opportunities for thinking and talking about the self in an authentic manner.

Many psychologists argue that people feel authentic when they are en-gaged in behavior that they enjoy for the sake of the activity itself, rather than as a means to external ends such as social prestige, acceptance, or money (Deci & Ryan, 1991). These kinds of activities are driven by intrin-sic motivation—internal needs to feel autonomous, competent, or close to other people. Studies have shown that college students who provide life nar-rative accounts featuring high levels of intrinsic motivation tend to enjoy concurrently higher levels of happiness and psychological well-being and show increases in well-being and happiness over time (McAdams, 2013). It would appear to follow that college students who take advantage of the Life Story Interview to explore their most authentic sources of meaning and pleasure might ultimately benefit the most from such an exercise.

Virtue: Living a Good Life.   In individualistic Western societies, liv-ing an authentic life is often seen as something good in itself. But even in those cultural contexts that encourage people most strongly to be them-selves and to do what they truly want to do, there is nonetheless recognition that people live in social groups and must adjust their behavior accordingly. Going back to Aristotle's (trans. 2004) *The Nicomachean Ethics*, the language of virtue identifies particular character traits that are deemed to be qualities of a good life because, for the most part, they enable people to live together well in groups. Indeed, Aristotle argued that citizens are happiest when they express virtues such as generosity, temperance, and friendship. The world's great religious traditions all enumerate characteristic virtues for good living. While each tradition identifies its own unique candidates, there is consider-able overlap for such virtues as honesty, fairness, love, self-control, humility, gratitude, and many others (Peterson & Seligman, 2004). Virtues are surely a subset of what William James referred to more generally as the "ideals" that come to be cultivated and explored during the college years (Schwehn & Bass, 2006).

The socialization of virtue begins in early childhood. In all human soci-eties, parents aim to instill virtues for good living, hoping that their children will get along well with others and attain some measure of social acceptance and status in life. The language of virtue may assume new urgency in the college years, however, as students come to question, or at least reexamine, the lessons of virtue they learned when they were younger. Erikson (1950) argued that the development of identity in late adolescence and young adulthood usually involves attaining some distance from the values, virtues, and ideologies that a young person learned growing up—beliefs about living a good life that have been reinforced by parents, churches, schools, and other socializing influences. Research shows that those college students who reexamine seriously the value systems that they internalized in earlier years tend to show higher levels of moral development and a more mature understanding of religious, political, and social issues, compared to their counterparts who fail to question (McAdams, 1985, 2013).

The Life Story Interview explicitly asks research participants to describe the fundamental beliefs and values that they hold in the realms of ethics, religion, and politics and to describe how those beliefs and values have changed over time. Because identity development in adolescence and young adulthood centrally concerns ideals and ideology, questions like these are arguably more relevant to the lives of many college students than they are to the midlife adults who typically participate in life-narrative research. Educators, counselors, and other college professionals, therefore, may find that the idea of constructing a story for one's life leads naturally to the consideration of what it means to live a life of virtue. The connection is perhaps easier to make at colleges and universities that are rooted in a religious tradition (Schwehn & Bass, 2006). However, secular institutions in the United States typically also ascribe to a set of values regarding how to live in a democratic society, implicitly urging students to embrace such virtues as honest inquiry, egalitarianism, social justice, tolerance, respect for diversity, and the like. Indeed, a tradition of explicating secular virtues in American society may be traced back to writings of Benjamin Franklin in the 18th century, if not further (McAdams, 2013). Many students want to know how to live a good life. The concept of narrative identity is broad enough to encompass this question. The Interview can, therefore, be a useful tool for the exploration and explication of human virtue.

Vocation: Making a Difference.   The concept of vocation finds its historical roots in the Protestant Reformation and Martin Luther's belief that all Christian men and women are "called" by God to service (Weber, 1904/1976). Luther and other Protestant theologians of the 16th and 17th centuries held that good works on earth were signs of a person's unique standing with God. As Luther saw it, any kind of regular and legitimate work—from manual labor to parenting to active involvement in the community—might qualify for the status of vocation, as long as the Christian did the work out of love for God and in service of humankind. In each person's own small way, therefore, he or she could make a positive difference in the world, while glorifying God in the process. In the 19th and 20th centuries, the concept of vocation evolved to encompass the more secular idea that each person may have unique talents and skills that can be used for the good of others, and it loosened its connection to religion.

On college campuses today, the language of vocation provides a strong alternative to the general sentiment that higher education should prepare young men and women to go out into the world to make money. Vocation is not necessarily antithetical to careerism and personal ambition, but it can soften and inform these motivations by adding the critical component of service. Many students find appealing the idea that the work they may do in life, whether in a volunteer capacity or for pay, may itself contribute to the betterment of others, even in small ways. The language of vocation is especially salient in such fields as teaching, medicine, and social work, but it can also inform how young people think about careers in business, engineering, law, and other areas. In recent years, colleges and universities have developed a range of programs to stimulate and support students' longing for vocation, from centers for civic engagement to leadership development programs. For example, Washington University in St. Louis sponsors leadership retreats wherein undergraduates explore how to position themselves in life so as to contribute, as leaders, to a more just, caring, and thriving world. In small groups, students draw up and discuss life maps, which diagram important areas of commitment and interest in their lives and project possible life trajectories through which personal vocation might be realized (Washington University, 2014).

Narrative identity encompasses a person's reconstruction of the past and imagined vision for the future. As people anticipate life chapters to come, they often incorporate into their story a *generativity script* (McAdams, 1985)—that is, a planned or imagined scenario whereby they hope to leave a positive legacy of the self for future generations. In the face of mortality, the generativity script sends this message: *Even though I will die, I have the opportunity to leave something positive behind. In the end, my life will have mattered. I will have made a difference.* Research suggests that life stories incorporating strong generativity scripts often adopt the language of vocation, sometimes going so far as to suggest that the protagonist of the story has been "chosen"—by God, by circumstances, by luck, by genes—to make a positive contribution to the world. Moreover, the most generative midlife adults in American society often tell stories about their lives that underscore the power of human *redemption* (McAdams, 2013). The protagonist often encounters setbacks and suffers many defeats, but negative events often give way to positive outcomes and meanings, as the suffering is repeatedly redeemed. In illustrating how the protagonist repeatedly overcomes adversity, these kinds of stories affirm the hope that hard work and suffering today will pay dividends in the future.

The Life Story Interview explicitly asks research participants to articulate a vision for the future and to explain how that future scenario may be linked to the past. As such, the interview offers an opportunity to think systematically about how one might find a vocation in life, drawing upon the rich storehouse of one's past experience to enable the protagonist to make a positive difference in the future. Although they face imposing stresses and potential obstacles to growth, college students have an opportunity to imagine a generative future that could be inspired by a vocation in life. Ideally, a student's story should reinforce who he or she truly is (authenticity) and how the student can live a good life (virtue). But it may also sustain hope of making a positive difference in the world (vocation), as the student embarks upon the journey of adulthood.

Conclusion

Many college students may find it useful to consider, in an explicit manner, the story of life that they are beginning to formulate as young adults who are about to enter the adult world of work, love, and commitment. Structured life storytelling and reflection, as developed in research on narrative identity and illustrated in the Life Story Interview, may raise new questions and open new ways of talking about ideals, work roles, and identity. Life storytelling may help students figure out what their real story is, how they may live a good life, and what they may need to do in the future in order to leave a positive mark in the world. By tapping into students' inchoate yearnings for authenticity, virtue, and vocation, life storytelling can complement other important experiences in school, both in the classroom and outside of it, in promoting and enhancing the search for identity in the college years.

References

Aristotle. (2004). *The Nicomachean ethics* (J. A. K. Thomson, Trans.; H. Tredennick, Ed.). London, England: Penguin.

Bruner, J. (1990). *Acts of meaning*. Cambridge, MA: Harvard University Press.

Deci, E., & Ryan, R. M. (1991). A motivational approach to self: Integration in personality. In R. Dienstbier & R. M. Ryan (Eds.), *Nebraska symposium on motivation* (Vol. 38, pp. 237–288). Lincoln: University of Nebraska Press.

Emerson, R. W. (1841/1993). *Self-reliance and other essays*. New York, NY: Dover.

Erikson, E. H. (1950). *Childhood and society*. New York, NY: Norton.

McAdams, D. P. (1985). *Power, intimacy, and the life story: Personological inquiries into identity*. Homewood, IL: Dorsey Press.

McAdams, D. P. (2013). *The redemptive self: Stories Americans live by* (revised and expanded edition). New York, NY: Oxford University Press.

McAdams, D. P., & McLean, K. C. (2013). Narrative identity. *Current Directions in Psychological Science, 22,* 233–238.

McLean, K. C., Pasupathi, M., & Pals, J. L. (2007). Selves creating stories creating selves: A process model of self-development. *Personality and Social Psychology Review, 11,* 262–278.

Peterson, C., & Seligman, M. E. P. (2004). *Character strengths and virtues: A handbook and classification*. New York, NY: Oxford University Press.

Schwehn, M. R., & Bass, D. C. (Eds.). (2006). *Leading lives that matter: What we should do and who we should be*. Grand Rapids, MI: William B. Eerdmans.

Taylor, C. (1991). *The ethics of authenticity*. Cambridge, MA: Harvard University Press.

Washington University. (2014). *Redefining community experience*. Retrieved from https://getinvolved.wustl.edu/get-involved/redefining-community-experience/Pages/default.aspx

Weber, M. (1904/1976). *The Protestant ethic and the spirit of capitalism* (T. Parsons, Trans.). New York, NY: Macmillan.

Dan P. McAdams is the Henry Wade Rogers Professor of Psychology and Human Development at Northwestern University.

Jennifer Guo is a doctoral student in the Psychology Department at Northwestern University.

New Directions for Higher Education • DOI: 10.1002/he

3

Developing self-authorship, or the internal capacity to construct one's beliefs, identity, and social relations, is crucial to successfully navigate adult life. Learning partnerships that engage collegians in interdependent relationships with educators support the transition from dependence on authority to self-authorship during college.

Self-Authorship

Marcia B. Baxter Magolda

The college experience is a time of transition. Whether it is a transition from adolescence to early adulthood for traditional-age students or a transition from one life path to another for older students, the college experience inevitably calls for reconsideration of one's role and responsibility in the world. College often coincides with the period Arnett (2006) calls emerging adulthood, which he describes as a space in between adolescence and young adulthood generally experienced between the ages of 18 to 25. Emerging adulthood is marked by identity exploration and opportunities for life transformation. Parks (2000) notes that between ages 17 and 30 young adults' meaning making shifts toward: "(1) becoming critically aware of one's own composing of reality, (2) self-consciously participating in an ongoing dialogue toward truth, and (3) cultivating a capacity to respond—to act—in ways that are satisfying and just" (p. 6). These perspectives, as well as those in the extensive literature on college student development, convey that the college experience is much more complicated than choosing a major and acquiring the knowledge and skills to succeed in a particular career path.

Today's college students are challenged to think critically in order to weigh relevant evidence to make sound decisions, craft a sense of identity that honors and balances their own and others' needs, and develop intercultural maturity to work interdependently with diverse others (Baxter Magolda & King, 2004; Kegan, 1994; King & Baxter Magolda, 2005). As leaders they will be expected to effectively manage conflict, ambiguity, change, and multiple perspectives (Berger, 2011; Drago-Severson, 2010; Kegan & Lahey, 2009). Thus while increasing their fund of knowledge and repertoire of skills during college is essential, this informational learning is insufficient to help collegians face the adaptive challenges of the 21st century. Adaptive challenges in which the problems and solutions are

New Directions for Higher Education, no. 166, Summer 2014 © 2014 Wiley Periodicals, Inc.
Published online in Wiley Online Library (wileyonlinelibrary.com) • DOI: 10.1002/he.20092

not clearly defined and are solved in the process of working through them require a shift in the ways we make sense of knowledge, our identities, and our social relations (Kegan & Lahey, 2009). This transformational learning, or shifting toward more complex ways of meaning making that enable managing ambiguity, is the core challenge of a college education that prepares graduates for productive lives as citizens of the larger world. To thrive in the ambiguity that characterizes contemporary adult life, collegians need to develop self-authorship, or the internal capacity to determine their beliefs, identities, and social relations (Baxter Magolda & King, 2004; Kegan 1994).

Research describes the nature of this transformation for both traditional-age and older adult learners as well as the role of culture and context in shaping it. Torres, Jones, and Renn (2009) summarized theories that portray identity as moving from simple to complex, socially constructed, and interactive with context. King (2009) synthesized cognitive and moral theories illustrating the principles and patterns of growth from uncritical reliance on external authority to establishing internal criteria for beliefs and moral judgment. Emphasizing Kegan's (1994) integration of cognitive, intrapersonal, and relational developmental dimensions, I synthesized holistic research on collegians' meaning making that portrays evolution from authority-dependence to self-authorship across the three dimensions (Baxter Magolda, 2009b). I find this holistic perspective most useful for understanding collegians' learning and development for two reasons: (a) it acknowledges that cognitive, identity, and relational development are inextricably intertwined; and (b) it blends psychological and sociological perspectives in recognizing that individuals construct meaning in context, shaped by and shaping the cultural and environmental systems with which they interact.

In this chapter, I offer one portrait of the journey toward self-authorship that emerged from my 27-year longitudinal study of young adults' development from age 18 to 45. The college phase included 80 traditional-age collegians who participated in in-depth annual interviews from 1986 to 1989 (Baxter Magolda, 1992); the postcollege phase includes 30 of those participants who continued to participate in annual interviews in their mid-forties (Baxter Magolda, 2001, 2009a). The overarching journey from uncritical reliance on external authority to self-authorship that emerged from this study also emerged in the Wabash National Study, in which 177 collegians from six diverse campuses participated in in-depth annual interviews from 2006 to 2009 (Baxter Magolda & King, 2012). I illustrate this portrait with one participant's story to help readers hear possibilities of how development evolves over time. I also describe the Learning Partnerships Model (LPM; Baxter Magolda, 2009a) that emerged from the longitudinal study to demonstrate how educational environments can be crafted to promote collegians' self-authorship.

NEW DIRECTIONS FOR HIGHER EDUCATION • DOI: 10.1002/he

The Journey Toward Self-Authorship

How collegians move from their socialization to rely on external authority toward establishing their internal authority depends on the dynamic interaction of their personal characteristics, experiences, their interpretation of those experiences, and their underlying constructions of knowledge, identity, and social relations (Baxter Magolda & King, 2012). Personal and environmental nuances, often related to experiencing marginalization, enable some collegians to shift toward self-authorship during college (Abes & Jones, 2004; Barber, King, & Baxter Magolda, 2013; King, Baxter Magolda, Joslin, & DeMonbrun, 2013; Pizzolato, 2003; Torres & Hernandez, 2007). However, most research reveals that traditional-age graduating seniors have yet to bring their internal voices to the foreground to coordinate external influence (Baxter Magolda, 1992; Baxter Magolda & King, 2012; King & Kitchener, 1994). My longitudinal participants relied on external authority during college, yet quickly began to question it soon after graduation when they encountered the demand for developing their internal voices. Gwen's story offers an example of this journey.

Uncritically Following External Formulas.   Gwen's education led her to gather knowledge from instructors when she entered college. She reported separating ideas in her notes during her first year so that she could visualize them in her mind for tests. By her second year she described using different color pens to see things more clearly. Gwen's focus on acquiring knowledge from an authority shifted in her junior year when her instructors began to interact with students, invite students' opinions, and encourage students to take a stand on ideas. Gwen described the impact of this new relationship:

> It's amazing how much different it is when you really are interested and involved. …because before you would read the material and be familiar with it and they'd tell you what to think, as opposed to now, when they say, "What do you think?" and you [say to yourself], "Oh, I'd better think of something." (Baxter Magolda, 1992, pp. 51–52)

This new approach to learning helped Gwen weigh opinions:

> As you hear more people's opinions, you piece together what you really think. Who has the valid point? Whose point is not valid in your opinion? And come to some other new understanding from a more dimensional perspective. It's super subjective. (Baxter Magolda, 1992, p. 59)

Although Gwen was learning to think for herself in these last two years of college (the cognitive dimension), she was still heavily reliant on external sources for career and personal decisions. She explained: "We're taught to make [our] plan. 'Plan your work and work your plan and you're going to get where you want to go.'" Taking this approach into her human relations position after graduation yielded surprising results:

> [I was] frustrated with not only a new job but also a new city and totally unfamiliar expectations. I hadn't had a chance to really get those ironed out, and basically they said, "We have faith in you; we think you can do this. Go ahead and do it." And I suddenly was saying, "Do what? What is it you want me to do?" ... I have actually found that what I learn through trial and error, although the process is a little bit more frustrating and a little bit more cumbersome in the beginning, I think I found better ways. I wasn't piggybacking off of what other people told me works that I may not find worked for myself. And I think I remembered it a lot better than having someone show me their way. Trying to figure out my way to do it, I think, was definitely better. (Baxter Magolda, 2001, pp. 43–44)

Learning to figure out how to function for herself at work and in her personal life, where she was struggling with whether to marry, led her to a crossroads.

Crossroads. The crossroads space is filled with tension between external influence and the growing internal voice as young adults work to make their own way in the world. Gwen articulated letting go of external formulas:

> I think in the past it was definitely, "What is protocol?" ... How does someone get from point A to point B? Because I could pretty much follow the rules to get there. If these are the things you need to do to be that, then I can do that and I can be that. I was pretty confident that that's how it worked. And now, thinking a little bit more outside the box, assuming I don't want to play by those rules because I can't, I have to look for a different way. It has definitely been an evolution for me. (Baxter Magolda, 2001, p. 50)

Recognizing that plans and protocol were insufficient for success in adult life brought Gwen face-to-face with uncertainty:

> I think my tendency whenever I make any big decision is to analyze to death and play out the "what ifs?" of every possible scenario. I about drive myself crazy doing that. ... [I have to] remember that I don't have to understand everything one hundred percent, that I don't have to have total and complete control over everything that touches me, that it's okay to go with the flow; it's okay to face the unknown. (Baxter Magolda, 2001, p. 48–49)

The intellectual awareness of facing uncertainty was easier than actually living with it, as was extracting oneself from others' expectations:

It's not that I'm letting go of the controlling and it's not that I'm saying that I don't feel compelled to do that, just that I'm better at managing it and better at understanding when to say when. And particularly as it applies to other people, ... I have a tendency to be so very concerned about other people's feelings that I let mine just totally go to pot. And I've tried to say, "Okay, I can be understanding and sympathetic and concerned about another's feelings, but take my sail out of their wind, so to speak. So that I hear you; you're not blowing me all over the place." So it's been a very powerful year for me ... and there's still a way to go; I'm not there yet. And that's something I'm probably going to work on for a long time. Because I can only control the way I feel. I really can't control how other people make me feel ... I guess understanding that there are limitations and you can't be all things to all people. Those are some pretty sobering realizations. Everybody—it's just human to want to be liked by a lot of people. And that everybody understands where you're coming from and appreciates your thoughts. And that's just not true. (Baxter Magolda, 2001, pp. 49–50)

Taking her sail out of others' wind meant bringing her internal voice to the foreground to coordinate external influence. Accepting that not everyone likes you or appreciates your thoughts, sobering as it was, enabled Gwen to move forward to self-author her life.

Self-Authorship.   Gwen's internal voice moved to the foreground in her mid-twenties as she took responsibility for her professional work and personal decisions. She described the change from her college experience:

I used to feel like I was on an out-of-control train ... it was driving me. Now I have a lot more control over where I'm going and the speed. It's wonderful. In college I was going to be married by 25. It's ironic. I used to be planned and that was debilitating. It's tied into understanding who I am. I remember in college, and in late teens, what others were doing was important, I never wanted to miss anything. You think you are independent, self-directed, but there's a lot of group think involved. The five or six years that follow college are critical years for learning. Get out of the structured atmosphere; try your own wings, fly on your own! What is supposed to be good, what is important to me, what are my real values? For the first time I have a chance to listen to my own voice. I finally got to a point [in my mid-twenties] where I was paying a lot of attention to that. ... During that time I was processing all that I had been gathering for the prior years. I was finally able to see a clear path, chart a course, and now am on the course. (Baxter Magolda, 2001, p. 59)

Gwen felt more content having chosen her own path:

I am much better, much more honest with myself, less inclined to base my actions and thoughts on what other people are telling me I should be doing or thinking. ...

> I probably feel more—not settled—but content with my life now than any other time I have talked to you. I struggle less. So probably, things we are talking about are a continuation of things I have found to be true rather than continuing to search. There is so much peace in just being rather than searching—frees you to enjoy so many other things. There are things that come up, but I have tools, I know how to handle them, so they are not as offsetting as they were. I roll with the punches better than ever … it's nice when you feel like home is portable. It is not external, it is inside relationships. This is a good place and I didn't get here overnight, so I appreciate it. (Baxter Magolda, 2001, p. 61)

This "good place" Gwen reached was internally constructing her beliefs, values, identity, and relationships, using her internal voice to coordinate the external influences in her life. This gave her the confidence to navigate life's adaptive challenges throughout her thirties and forties.

Learning Partnerships

As Gwen's journey illustrates, the internal voice begins to emerge when external others encourage it to come forward or when relying uncritically on external formulas stops working. Gwen's college instructors initiated this in her junior year and her postgraduation work setting demanded it more explicitly. My longitudinal participants' descriptions of the challenges and supports that helped them move through the crossroads and into self-authorship yielded the Learning Partnerships Model (Baxter Magolda, 2009a). Learning partners support learners' internal voices by

- respecting their thoughts and feelings, thus affirming the value of their voices;
- helping them view their experiences as opportunities for learning and growth; and
- collaborating with them to analyze their own problems, engaging in mutual learning with them. (Baxter Magolda, 2009a, p. 251)

Learning partners challenge learners to develop self-authorship by

- drawing participants' attention to the complexity of their work and life decisions, and discouraging simplistic solutions;
- encouraging participants to develop their personal authority by listening to their own voices in determining how to live their lives; and

- encouraging participants to share authority and expertise, and work interdependently with others to solve mutual problems. (Baxter Magolda, 2009a, p. 251)

Grounding learning partnerships in learners' thoughts, feelings, and experiences welcomes all learners' personal characteristics and contextual circumstances. Interdependent learning and problem solving in which educators share authority with learners guide learners in refining their internal voices to construct their beliefs, values, identities, and social relations. Numerous examples of successful learning partnerships in a wide range of contexts (e.g., courses, academic programs, advising, orientation, residential life, learning assistance, and leadership programs) and with a wide range of student populations demonstrate that learners' internal voices can be cultivated earlier in college (for detailed descriptions of these innovations, see Baxter Magolda & King, 2004; Meszaros, 2007; Pizzolato, 2006; Taylor, Baxter Magolda, & Haynes, 2010).

These examples reveal that engaging in learning partnerships requires that educators relinquish control in order to share authority, trust learners' capabilities, navigate ambiguity in partnerships that are more fluid, and develop the complex cognitive, intrapersonal, and interpersonal capacities to interact interdependently with diverse learners.

Future Research

Sufficient evidence exists that self-authorship supports critical thinking, complex problem solving, mature relationships, intercultural maturity, leadership, and navigating life challenges. Evidence that learning partnerships enable collegians to develop self-authorship warrants reform of higher education to accelerate learners' internal voices. Yet many college environments do not afford learners learning partnerships that welcome their voices. An important focus for future research is how to alter college environments to engage college students as adults. How can policy be altered such that it affords learners an appropriate balance of autonomy and responsibility to the campus community? How can peer culture be reshaped to encourage less reliance on what others' think? How can learners' expectations about their role in learning be reshaped such that they are able to participate in learning partnerships? How can educators be supported in altering their assumptions about and relationships with learners? How can educators be supported in their own developmental growth to achieve capacities for interdependence? How can we help all constituents to realize the important role of developmental capacity in the educated person? Delving into these intricacies is crucial to reshaping the college experience to promote the internal voice we know young adults need to navigate the complexities of adult life. We have "a responsibility to help young adults make the transition from being shaped by society to shaping society" (Baxter Magolda, 1999, p. 630).

References

Abes, E. S., & Jones, S. R. (2004). Meaning-making capacity and the dynamics of lesbian college students' multiple dimensions of identity. *Journal of College Student Development*, *45*(6), 612–632.

Arnett, J. J. (2006). Emerging adulthood: Understanding a new way of coming of age. In J. J. Arnett & J. L. Tanner (Eds.), *Emerging adults in America: Coming of age in the 21st century* (pp. 3–19). Washington DC: American Psychological Association.

Barber, J., King, P. M., & Baxter Magolda, M. B. (2013). Long strides in the journey toward self-authorship: Substantial developmental shifts in college students' meaning making. *Journal of Higher Education*, *84*(6), 866–895.

Baxter Magolda, M. B. (1992). *Knowing and reasoning in college: Gender-related patterns in students' intellectual development*. San Francisco, CA: Jossey-Bass.

Baxter Magolda, M. B. (1999). Constructing adult identities. *Journal of College Student Development*, *40*(6), 629–644.

Baxter Magolda, M. B. (2001). *Making their own way: Narratives for transforming higher education to promote self-development*. Sterling, VA: Stylus.

Baxter Magolda, M. B. (2009a). *Authoring your life: Developing an internal voice to navigate life's challenges*. Sterling, VA: Stylus.

Baxter Magolda, M. B. (2009b). The activity of meaning making: A holistic perspective on college student development. *Journal of College Student Development*, *50*(6), 621–639.

Baxter Magolda, M. B., & King, P. M. (Eds.). (2004). *Learning partnerships: Theory & models of practice to educate for self-authorship*. Sterling, VA: Stylus.

Baxter Magolda, M. B., & King, P. M. (2012). Assessing meaning making and self-authorship: Theory, research, and application. *ASHE Higher Education Report*, *38*(3). San Francisco, CA: Jossey-Bass.

Berger, J. G. (2011). *Changing on the job: Developing leaders for a complex world*. Stanford, CA: Stanford University Press.

Drago-Severson, E. (2010). *Leading adult learning*. Thousand Oaks, CA: Corwin.

Kegan, R. (1994). *In over our heads: The mental demands of modern life*. Cambridge, MA: Harvard University Press.

Kegan, R., & Lahey, L. L. (2009). *Immunity to change: How to overcome it and unlock potential in yourself and your organization*. Boston, MA: Harvard Business Press.

King, P. M. (2009). Principles of development and developmental change underlying theories of cognitive and moral development. *Journal of College Student Development*, *50*(6), 597–639.

King, P. M., & Baxter Magolda, M. B. (2005). A developmental model of intercultural maturity. *Journal of College Student Development*, *46*(6), 571–592.

King, P. M., Baxter Magolda, M. B., Joslin, J. Y., & DeMonbrun, M. (2013, November). *Self-authoring seniors*. Paper presented at the Association for the Study of Higher Education, St. Louis, MO.

King, P. M., & Kitchener, K. S. (1994). *Developing reflective judgment: Understanding and promoting intellectual growth and critical thinking in adolescents and adults*. San Francisco, CA: Jossey-Bass.

Meszaros, P. S. (Ed.). (2007). *New Directions for Teaching and Learning: No. 109. Self-authorship: Advancing students' intellectual growth*. San Francisco, CA: Jossey-Bass.

Parks, S. D. (2000). *Big questions, worthy dreams: Mentoring young adults in their search for meaning, purpose, and faith*. San Francisco, CA: Jossey-Bass.

Pizzolato, J. E. (2003). Developing self-authorship: Exploring the experiences of high-risk college students. *Journal of College Student Development, 44*(6), 797–812.

Pizzolato, J. E. (2006). Complex partnerships: Self-authorship and provocative academic advising practices. *NACADA Journal, 26*(1), 32–45.

Taylor, K. B., Baxter Magolda, M. B., & Haynes, C. (2010). Miami University's collective journey toward discovery-based learning. *Learning Communities Journal, Special Issue, 2*(2), 1–26.

Torres, V., & Hernandez, E. (2007). The influence of ethnic identity development on self-authorship: A longitudinal study of Latino/a college students. *Journal of College Student Development, 48*(5), 558–573.

Torres, V., Jones, S. R., & Renn, K. A. (2009). Identity development theories in student affairs: Origins, current status, and new approaches. *Journal of College Student Development, 50*(6), 577–596.

MARCIA B. BAXTER MAGOLDA is a distinguished professor of educational leadership at Miami University (Ohio).

4

The dominant paradigm in the literature of college student development reflects a cognitive or psychological bias when considering the effect that college has on students. This chapter offers an alternative perspective by recognizing college as a social process and subsequently examines students' identity formation from a sociological perspective.

The Sociology of College Students' Identity Formation

Peter Kaufman

When we consider the effect that college has on the development of students, we often think in terms of psychological or cognitive changes. Indeed, for over 40 years the majority of research on college students has tended to examine the outcome of the college experience almost exclusively from the perspective of the individual (see Feldman, 1972; Pascarella & Terenzini, 1991, 2005). The fallacy with this approach is that college is not an individual experience; rather, it is a social experience. One might even say it is a social process. As such, if we want to have a more complete understanding of the impact of the undergraduate experience it seems necessary that we incorporate a social analysis into the preponderance of psychological and cognitive research. In this chapter, I argue for the importance of a social analysis of the college experience. Specifically, I examine how college impacts the formation of a college student's identity. Although identity is often posited as an individually based achievement, I use the sociological theory of symbolic interaction to explain how it is more appropriate to understand identity formation as a process of both personal avowals and social attributions. I conclude by suggesting future avenues of research as well as considerations for those who work closely with college students.

A Brief Primer on Symbolic Interaction

Symbolic interaction is a theoretical perspective within sociology that focuses predominantly on the interactional processes of social life (Charon, 2009). Emerging from the philosophical tradition of American pragmatism, symbolic interactionists are largely concerned with human conduct, the

NEW DIRECTIONS FOR HIGHER EDUCATION, no. 166, Summer 2014 © 2014 Wiley Periodicals, Inc.
Published online in Wiley Online Library (wileyonlinelibrary.com) • DOI: 10.1002/he.20093

construction and maintenance of meaning, and the extent to which individuals situate themselves as both subjects and objects of social action. The term symbolic interaction was coined by Herbert Blumer (1969) who outlined three premises of this theoretical perspective:

> The first premise is that human beings act toward things on the basis of the meanings that the things have for them. The second premise is that the meaning of such things is derived from, or arises out of, social interaction. The third premise is that these meanings are handled in, and modified through, an interpretive process. (p. 2)

The majority of the sociological literature pertaining to self and identity grows out of the symbolic interactionist tradition. Individuals are viewed as social constructions—as becoming who they are more from nurture (external, social factors) than from nature (internal, biopsychological factors). Sociologists attempt to understand identity formation by situating the individual in a particular social world because it is the interactions in social settings that construct who we are. As George Herbert Mead (1934) argued, we come to understand who we are and form a self-definition by embracing the attitudes of the significant others with whom we interact. Symbolic interactionists also make the point that we commonly take the ascriptions and attributions that others make of us and internalize them as part of our identity (Rosenberg, 1981). Mead spoke specifically about this process as taking on the roles of others and having the ability to see oneself reflexively—from the perspective of others. In the identity formation process, the individual eventually learns to embrace the role of the generalized other and forms a more complete picture of himself or herself in the larger social world. This more complete sense of self incorporates the attitude of the entire group to which the individual belongs.

Mead's concept of the generalized other is crucial to the conception of the self as being socially rooted—as in a college environment, for example. Even the famous developmental psychologist Erik Erikson (1968), coming out of the psychoanalytic tradition, recognized the importance of locating the individual in the social setting. He suggested that identity development is a psychosocial process not centered solely around the individual but also situated in the heart of the communal culture. According to Erikson, traditional psychoanalytic theory is unable to grasp a true sense of identity because of its inability to account for the *umwelt*—the external environment that both surrounds us and is in us. Since members of the same culture share the same *umwelt* this concept serves for Erikson a similar purpose as Mead's (1934) generalized other. Both represent the social setting the individual has internalized and which influences the individual's perception of self and others.

When the individual is able to take on the role of the generalized other she or he is also able to send and receive gestures. Gestures represent symbols that link the individual to the social group. When the receiver of a gesture interprets it as the gesture was intended to be interpreted by the sender, Mead (1934) calls this language. Language in this sense may be understood literally, as a system of voice sounds, or figuratively, as a system of attitudes, meanings, and dispositions. Either way, it functions as the mechanism through which an individual forms an identity. It is through language that one becomes a member of a community by taking the "institutions of that community into his [or her] conduct" (p. 162). A prerequisite to identity formation then is locating oneself within a social group and, more importantly, internalizing the dispositions of that group.

With its focus on social interaction and the embracement of the group's attitudes, it should not be surprising that the symbolic interactionist approach to studying identity is more focused on social identity than personal identity. Personal identity is commonly understood as avowals or self-declarations: I am a good student, I am a friendly person, and I am hard working. Personal identity often falls more under the purview of the psychological development literature on student identity. In contrast, social identity is based on the imputations that others make toward us. Social identity emerges from the interplay of the individual and collective (Jenkins, 1997; Stets & Burke, 2000). It is one thing to feel that you are a friendly or hard-working college student, but unless others ascribe or reflect this identity back to you it is unlikely that your self-avowals will go very far. In this sense, social identity may be said to be a more accurate description of who we are.

Symbolic Interaction and College Student Identity Formation

So how does the symbolic interactionist approach to identity formation play out in the college environment? It should be clear from the preceding summary that college is an important social location where identity formation occurs. As a location of social interaction at a time when individuals are moving from one developmental stage (young adulthood) into another (adulthood), college is a crucial site whereby individuals strive to find consistency between their personal identity (self-avowals) and their social identity (ascriptions from others). Seeing college as a social institution where students' identities are constructed through social interaction is an important framework for faculty and professional staff. College is not just an arena for intellectual development and advancement; additionally, it is a site in which students construct a sense of self that situates them in a particular social location with a set of corresponding social roles. Let me briefly offer a concrete example of college students' identity formation from some of my own research.

Education has always been viewed as the medium through which individuals can achieve upward social mobility. Whether or not this is true, there is no denying that individuals who have a bachelor's degree are more

NEW DIRECTIONS FOR HIGHER EDUCATION • DOI: 10.1002/he

likely than those without a college degree to hold professional, middle-class occupations. For this reason, we may say that college is instrumental in preparing students for a professional lifestyle—even if this is not an explicitly stated goal of an institution's mission statement. Stated alternatively, we may say that the college experience helps students construct a specific class-based identity. In some of my own work (Kaufman, 2003, 2005; Kaufman & Feldman, 2004), I demonstrate how students construct their class-based identities in college. Students who are first-generation college students as well as those from middle- or upper-class backgrounds must actively construct a class-based identity that is reflected back to them by significant others. College is the prime location where students begin the transition from the role of student to the role of professional.

This identity formation process is somewhat easier for students who already exist in middle- or upper-class locations, but it is no less active, no less devoid of agency, than for students from lower social classes. In all cases, one's personal identity will not stick unless it is certified by having others reflect that identity back to the individual. In this sense, all students who are striving to have a certain class-based identity imputed to them must engage in identity-work activities to ensure that they achieve this desired social psychological result. The sociologist Erving Goffman (1967), whose work is central to the symbolic interactionist tradition even though Goffman himself rejected this label, explained the interplay between personal identity and social identity as such: "While his social face [identity] can be his most personal possession and the center of his security and pleasure, it is only on loan to him from society; it will be withdrawn unless he conducts himself in a way that is worthy of it" (p. 10). All of us no doubt have experienced what Goffman is getting at in this passage. For college students hoping to construct an identity that will propel them into the future, the stakes are obviously quite high and therefore it is necessary that faculty and staff recognize their role in this identity-formation process.

In my research, the identity-work strategies I focused on revolved around how students aligned themselves with certain groups or individuals and how they distanced themselves from others. Seeking categorical membership in a social group is a key component of social identity formation, and I examined how students achieved this through such dimensions as choosing a particular style of dress, employing specific speech patterns, and seeking out various leisure activities. Many students were consciously aware of how they altered or adopted certain ways of dressing, speaking, and socializing so that they were conducting themselves in a manner that was worthy of their desired social identity. The key point to keep in mind from a symbolic interactionist position is that students in college form their identities by taking on the attitude of the group to which they aspire to belong. From this angle, the college experience is significant not only because of how students develop intellectually or emotionally; rather, college is also important because it plays a significant role in the construction of a class-based identity that situates individuals into socioeconomic positions.

My work was specifically on social-class identity formation, but the symbolic interactionist approach has wide applicability for understanding the college experience. For example, this sociological perspective is commonly used in the context of other social indicators such as race and ethnicity and gender and sexuality. In much the same way that students engage in identity-work strategies to solidify their desired social-class identity, college is also fertile ground in which students cement their identities along the lines of race, ethnicity, gender, and sexuality. Through their social interactions with peers, faculty, and staff, students learn to take the attitude of others with regard to these social locations. They learn what it means to identify and differentiate themselves as Black, Latino, bisexual, or even straight, and they work to behave in ways so that these identities are acknowledged and accepted by significant others.

Moving beyond the formation of identities based on these social variables, the symbolic interactionist perspective is useful for those who are interested in trying to better understand the college experience because it focuses specifically on the ways in which college students construct meanings—particularly about self and other. Whereas typical cognitive assessments ostensibly measure whether or not students are gaining intellect, the symbolic interactionist approach considers whether or not students identify as being intellectual. Administrators and policy makers who are motivated solely by number-based outcome assessments will not be particularly interested in this element of a college student's felt identity; however, the importance of understanding this process cannot be overstated. One of the major limitations of the current focus on cognitive assessment and psychological development is that it fails to see college students as whole persons. We are so focused on measuring *what* students are learning that we have given very little attention to *who* they are becoming. Students are not just going out into the world as containers of discipline-specific knowledge. They are also going into the world as individuals in the throes of important identity development. Symbolic interaction is distinctly suited to studying this process.

Studying the Impact of College Through Symbolic Interaction: Future Directions

By way of concluding this chapter, I offer two examples of implementing the symbolic interactionist approach described here: (a) a proposal for research and (b) a suggestion for faculty and staff who interact regularly with college students.

In terms of possible research, much could be gained by more ethnographic accounts of the college student experience. This methodological

approach—whether it be based on participant observation or nonparticipant observation—is ideally suited to the theoretical position of symbolic
interaction. Much like symbolic interaction, ethnographers study social interaction, the social construction of reality, and the production and reproduction of shared norms—all of which are building blocks for a student's
identity formation. Although there is a long and rich tradition of ethnographic studies of primary and secondary schools (see, e.g., Foley, 2010;
Khan, 2010; Lareau, 2000; Lewis, 2003; MacLeod, 2009; Thorne, 1993;
Willis, 1977), there is a noticeable dearth of similar work at the college
level (for two exceptions see Moffatt, 1989; Nathan, 2005). If we accept the
basic symbolic interactionist premise that "human society consists of people engaging in action" (Blumer, 1969, p. 7) then we surely need greater
insight into the myriad of social interactions that occur in the daily life of
college students. We need a better understanding of how students exchange
gestures, how they take on the role of others, and how they see themselves
as objects to themselves. Studying college students through the theoretical
lens of symbolic interaction and the methodological perspective of ethnography gets at these important themes.

Symbolic interaction also provides instructive guidance for our daily
interactions with students. With the awareness that all of our interactions serve as the foundation for the production and reproduction of identities, faculty and staff might be less cavalier and more sympathetic to
students. I am not suggesting that it is necessarily common for faculty
and staff to be dismissive of students; however, the recognition that students may be trying out identities and making avowals that they hope to
be reciprocated as ascriptions might elicit a deeper level of understanding and attention among faculty and staff. As a specific example, consider
the importance of student–faculty research collaborations. As Posselt and
Black (2012) demonstrate, these ongoing interactions may contribute significantly to the formation of a professional identity among students—
particularly first-generation college students. Faculty interactions in the
classroom, during office hours, at extracurricular events as well as staff
interactions with students in administrative offices and service centers
are similarly poised to be potential occasions of college students' identity
formation.

In his theoretical explanation of symbolic interaction, Herbert Blumer
(1969) notes that life is a formative and unfolding process; it is not just
the arena for human expression. He goes on to say that human beings are
acting organisms and not mere responding organisms. These are important
themes to keep in mind. Too much of the research on college student development approaches students as responding organisms—responding to
cognitive and psychological assessments—so that we can see how they express themselves along these dimensions. A focus on the *process* of the college experience, as well as on college students' identity formation, is still
untapped in the college development literature. There is a greater need to

understand college as an unfolding process in which students act toward themselves and others based on the socially constructed meanings of their actions. The sociological theory of symbolic interaction is ideally suited to studying this process and providing further insights into college students' identity formation.

References

Blumer, H. (1969). *Symbolic interaction: Perspective and method.* Berkeley: University of California Press.

Charon, J. M. (2009). *Symbolic interaction: An introduction, an interpretation, an integration.* New York, NY: Pearson.

Erikson, E. (1968). *Identity: Youth and crisis.* New York, NY: W.W. Norton & Company.

Feldman, K. A. (1972). Some theoretical approaches to the study of change and stability of college students. *Review of Educational Research, 42*(1), 1–26.

Foley, D. E. (2010). *Learning capitalist culture* (2nd ed.). Philadelphia: University of Pennsylvania Press.

Goffman, E. (1967). *Interaction ritual: Essays on face-to-face behavior.* New York, NY: Pantheon.

Jenkins, R. (1997). *Social identity.* London, England: Routledge.

Kaufman, P. (2003). Learning to not labor: How working-class individuals construct middle-class identities. *The Sociological Quarterly, 44*(3), 481–504.

Kaufman, P. (2005). Middle-class social reproduction: The activation and negotiation of structural advantages. *Sociological Forum, 20*(2), 245–270.

Kaufman, P., & Feldman, K. A. (2004). Forming identities in college: A sociological approach. *Research in Higher Education, 45*(5), 463–496.

Khan, S. R. (2010). *Privilege: The making of an adolescent elite at St. Paul's School.* Princeton, NJ: Princeton University Press.

Lareau, A. (2000). *Home advantage: Social class and parental intervention in elementary education.* Lanham, MD: Rowman & Littlefield.

Lewis, A. E. (2003). *Race in the school yard: Negotiating the color line in classrooms and communities.* New Brunswick, NJ: Rutgers University Press.

MacLeod, J. (2009). *Ain't no makin' it: Aspirations and attainment in a low-income neighborhood* (3rd ed.). Boulder, CO: Westview Press.

Mead, G. H. (1934). *Mind, self, and society.* Chicago, IL: University of Chicago Press.

Moffatt, M. (1989). *Coming of age in New Jersey: College and American culture.* New Brunswick, NJ: Rutgers University Press.

Nathan, R. [C. A. Small]. (2005). *My freshman year: What a professor learned by becoming a student.* Ithaca, NY: Cornell University Press.

Pascarella, E. T., & Terenzini, P. T. (1991). *How college affects students: Findings and insights from twenty years of research.* San Francisco, CA: Jossey-Bass.

Pascarella, E. T., & Terenzini, P. T. (2005). *How college affects students: A third decade of research.* San Francisco, CA: Jossey-Bass.

Posselt, J. R., & Black, K. R. (2012). Developing the research identities and aspirations of first-generation college students: Evidence from the McNair scholars program. *International Journal for Researcher Development, 3*(1), 26–48.

Rosenberg, M. (1981). The self-concept: Social product and social force. In M. Rosenberg & R. Turner (Eds.), *Social psychology: Sociological perspectives* (pp. 593–624). New York, NY: Basic Books.

Stets, J. E., & Burke, P. J. (2000). Identity theory and social identity theory. *Social Psychology Quarterly, 63*(3), 224–237.

Thorne, B. (1993). *Gender play: Girls and boys in school.* New Brunswick, NJ: Rutgers University Press.

Willis, P. (1977). *Learning to labor.* New York, NY: Columbia University Press.

PETER KAUFMAN *is an associate professor of sociology at the State University of New York, New Paltz.*

5

This chapter describes the contribution of current research using the Weidman model of undergraduate socialization to understanding student identity development in college. It illustrates ways in which the framework can be used flexibly and adapted for studying impacts of multiple aspects of the college experience on diverse groups of students.

Understanding Student Identity From a Socialization Perspective

John C. Weidman, Linda DeAngelo, Kathryn A. Bethea

The chapter begins with a brief description of the Weidman (1989) model of undergraduate socialization, showing its evolution over the past three decades and its changing application in published research and scholarship. We then review a set of recently published articles focusing on student development outcomes. We describe how social relationships in college, including membership in diverse social, economic, gender, and ethnic/racial groups, are related to identity development. We conclude by showing how the Weidman model can be used to frame research on college student identity.

Evolution of the Weidman Model

According to Jones and Abes (2013), student development theory and the study of identity is organized around three domains—cognitive, interpersonal, and intrapersonal. Because the Weidman (1989) socialization model focuses on college experience and development in these domains, reviewing and conducting studies that use the model can inform our understanding of identity development in college and assist practitioners to develop programs and practices aimed at assisting students with building a strong sense of self.

   The first published version of the Weidman model appeared in an empirical study of the impact of college experiences on undergraduates' career choices (Weidman, 1984). Formulated using sociological perspectives, the model's conceptual starting point is a definition of socialization as "the process by which persons acquire the knowledge, skills, and dispositions that

NEW DIRECTIONS FOR HIGHER EDUCATION, no. 166, Summer 2014 © 2014 Wiley Periodicals, Inc.
Published online in Wiley Online Library (wileyonlinelibrary.com) • DOI: 10.1002/he.20094

Figure 5.1. The Weidman (1989) Model of Undergraduate Socialization

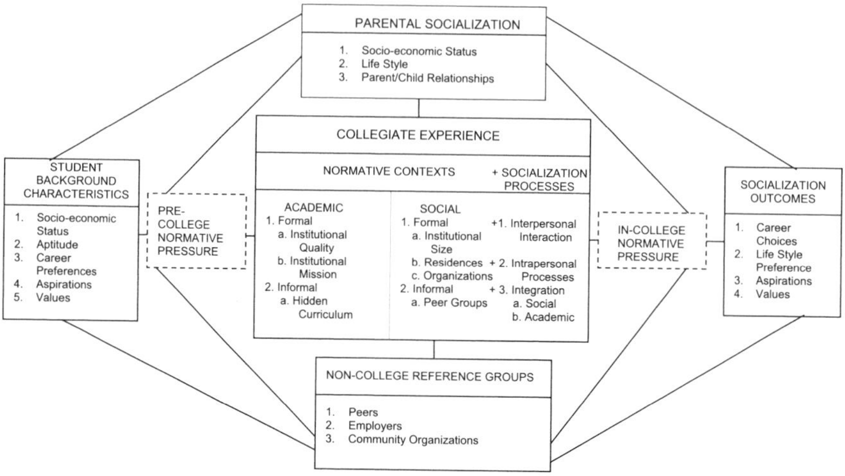

Source: Weidman (1989). Reprinted with kind permission from Springer Science+Business Media B.V.

make them more or less effective members of their society" (Brim, 1966, p. 3). In contrast to the prevalent view in research on college impact in the early 1980s, this framework included specific consideration of potential influences outside the college, asserting that higher education institutions should not be thought of as encapsulated environments. During college, students continue to remain in periodic contact with, and are influenced by, significant others outside their higher education institutions, such as parents, other relatives, and friends (Weidman, 1984).

An expanded version of the model was published in a conceptually focused literature review (Weidman, 1989). The elaborated model, shown in Figure 5.1, incorporates notions of norms and social relationships reflected in academic and social contexts that had been published earlier in the work on higher education attrition by Spady (1970) and Tinto (1975). In addition to social integration, the 1989 version also includes interpersonal interaction and intrapersonal socialization processes. To summarize, the Weidman framework reflects an underlying conceptualization of undergraduate socialization as a series of experiences and processes occurring as the student:

1. enters college as a freshman with certain values, aspirations, and other personal goals;
2. is exposed to various socializing influences while attending college, including normative pressures exerted via (a) social relationships with

college faculty and peers, (b) parental pressures, and (c) involvement with noncollege reference groups;

3. assesses the salience of the various normative pressures encountered for attaining personal goals; and

4. changes or maintains those values, aspirations, and personal goals that were held at college entrance.

In this framework (Weidman, 1989), normative contexts are settings in which students are exposed to ideas and perspectives shaped by experiences with value-laden structures, such as academic disciplines/fields of study or more informal experiences with peers, cocurricular organizations, or faculty outside of formal class settings. Primary socialization processes include interpersonal relationships (peer and faculty interaction), intrapersonal/learning activities (studying and attending lectures), and integration (incorporation into campus academic and social life).

Recognized for its conceptual significance, Weidman's (1989) work was cited in other major student development sources (Bess, 1991; Bess & Webster, 1999; Chickering & Reisser, 1993) and was reprinted in Pascarella & Terenzini's (1991, 2005) *How College Affects Students*. Overall, however, the model had little early use in research on college undergraduate student development. Meanwhile, the model was applied to graduate student socialization (Weidman, Twale, & Stein, 2001), and a further elaboration was published five years later (Weidman, 2006) that included cognitive (knowledge) and psychomotor (skills) as well as affective outcomes.

The Weidman Model in Current Research on College Student Development

In order to assess how Weidman's (1989) model of undergraduate socialization has been used in recent years to enhance understanding of student identity development, we first identified a set of 17 articles and chapters published between 2003 and 2013 that used the model explicitly in research design and interpretation of results. Several focus on diverse populations (Antonio, 2004; Carter, Locks, & Winkle-Wagner, 2013; Cole, 2011; Davis et al., 2010; Eagan et al., 2013; Espinosa, 2011; Holley & Taylor, 2009; Inkelas, 2003; Johnson, 2012), and two explore the role of parental influences during college (Agliata & Renk, 2008; Sax & Wartman, 2010). Other topics addressed include civic values (Lott, 2013), social networking (Corwin & Cintrón, 2011), and student retention (Titus, 2004).

We focus in this chapter on six empirical studies published between 2003 and 2013 that used the Weidman (1989) framework. The developmental outcomes studied in the reviewed articles include intellectual self-confidence and degree aspirations (Antonio, 2004), intellectual self-concept and college GPA (Cole, 2011), pluralistic orientation (Engberg, 2007), engagement with faculty mentors (Fuentes, Alvarado, Berdan, & DeAngelo,

2013), sense of belonging (Johnson, 2012), and desire to participate in complex cognitive activities (Padgett et al., 2010).

Three of these articles (Cole, 2011; Fuentes et al., 2013; Padgett et al., 2010) address the role of faculty in student development. Fuentes et al. studied the relationship between early faculty contact outside of the classroom and later mentorship. They found that early interaction with faculty and accompanying student integration into the normative contexts of those interactions is essential to the formation of mentoring relationships with faculty later in students' college careers. Early socialization experiences were especially important for students whose intrapersonal sense of self in relation to faculty at the beginning of college was not likely to lead directly to the fostering of mentoring relationships. Still, the benefits of student–faculty interaction in the first year of college were unequal. Although students who had not declared a major at the beginning of college were more likely to interact with faculty in the first year of college, they were less likely to have mentoring relationships with faculty in their senior year of college. Additionally, students who attended less selective institutions were less likely to be mentored in the senior year despite having more interaction with faculty in their first year.

Padgett et al. (2010) also found a conditional effect related to student–faculty interaction. In studying the desire of students to engage in complex cognitive activities (need for cognition), they found that quality of nonclassroom interactions with faculty (perceived influence on personal growth, intellectual growth, and career goals; having a personal relationship with at least one faculty member; and satisfaction with opportunities to interact informally) was negatively related to need for cognition for first-generation students. Thus, despite the finding that quality of nonclassroom interactions with faculty was positive overall, for this group of students those same interactions did not increase the complexity of their cognitive activities.

In fact, as Padgett et al. (2010) discuss, those who score lower on need for cognition are more likely to rely on external influences, in this case faculty, to help them make sense of their world. The movement from the source of knowledge as being external to oneself as opposed to internal is one of the key components of developing self-authorship (Baxter Magolda, 2001). This finding suggests that even though first-generation students view the quality of their interaction with faculty the same as other students, the nature of that interaction is different. Consequently, non-first-generation students engage in further cognitive complexity and a journey toward self-authorship in the cognitive domain while their first-generation peers do not advance as far in this domain. The mixed findings with respect to the impact of student–faculty interaction in both studies lend credence to Weidman's (1984, 1989) claim that primary social relationships have strong socializing influences and that it is not just frequency of student–faculty interaction but also the intensity and quality of these relationships that make a difference.

Cole (2011), in a study examining intellectual self-concept and college GPA for African-American students, finds a positive effect of informal interaction with faculty on both of these outcomes. Despite this, the overall gains in intellectual self-concept among African-American students between the beginning and end of college are so small that Cole concludes the sense of academic identity for this particular group is already well established before they start college. Thus, although interaction with faculty and peers in the college environment has a positive relationship with academic achievement, African-American students have a concept of self at college entry that stays largely unchanged during college despite the interpersonal interaction and integration experiences, both positive and negative, these students might have during college. This finding supports Weidman's (1989) assertion that the model is sufficiently general to include assessment of variations in socialization experiences by gender, racial, and ethnic group.

Antonio (2004) focuses specifically on college peer groups as a source of informal socialization. This study explores the connection between the socialization processes occurring within peer groups (characterized by racial diversity, academic abilities, and aspirations) and changes during college in intellectual self-confidence and degree aspirations. Antonio found that students in diverse friendship groups had higher degree aspirations than students in homogenous friendship groups. This suggests that interpersonal interaction in heterogeneous friendship groups generated strong normative pressure that, in turn, led to higher degree aspirations. This may have occurred through a changing sense of self in the intrapersonal dynamics these interactions created. Interestingly, for White students these intrapersonal processes may have had leveled out their sense of self in relation to diverse others. Results also showed that White students in diverse peer groups had lower self-confidence and degree aspirations overall than did White students with similar characteristics who were in homogenous peer groups. The reverse was true for students of color. Using Weidman's model as a frame to understand the socialization process during college, this study demonstrates the importance of frequent, primary relationships.

Focusing on socialization experiences in diverse environments, Engberg (2007) studied changes in pluralistic orientation (the dispositions and skills needed for working in a diverse workforce) among students in the first two years of college. The major finding of the study was that intergroup learning, an intrapersonal socialization process in Weidman's model, was directly related to gains in pluralistic orientation skills. Modeling further showed that students who had positive interactions across race were more likely to show growth in intergroup learning, and that positive interactions across race were connected to the college normative context as measured by student body diversity. Thus, the formal institutional normative context facilitated the socialization process through interpersonal interaction across race that, in turn, facilitated intrapersonal learning leading to gains in pluralistic orientation skills.

Engberg's (2007) study also found that the largest effect on inter-group learning was student participation in cocurricular diversity program-ming, an additional normative context. From this he concludes the learning occurring in these experiences is central to gains in pluralistic orientation for all students, but only to the extent these experiences engage students as willing participants in learning more about their own social identity as well as the social identities of diverse others. These findings correspond directly with the multiple socialization processes described in the Weidman (1989) model.

Finally, Johnson (2012) addresses sense of belonging among women in STEM (science, technology, engineering, and mathematics) majors. The study contributes to our understanding of the effect of informal socializa-tion experiences (both inter- and intrapersonal) in college contexts reflect-ing ways in which different dimensions of the institutional climate (res-idence halls and campus as a whole) may influence student development. For the diverse group of women studied, perceptions of an academically and socially supportive residence hall climate were the largest determinants of their sense of belonging, with perceptions of a positive racial climate on campus of almost equal importance.

The study also found that despite equally positive perceptions of aca-demic and social support in the residence halls and a positive racial cli-mate on campus, sense of belonging was lower for women of color than for White women. As Johnson (2012) suggests, for women of color, the intra-personal processes driving their perceptions of the racial climate on cam-pus may be more important to sense of belonging than for White women due to the confluence of their social identities as both women and women of color. This conclusion is consistent with an understanding of multiple social identities as seen through the lens of intersectionality (Dill, McLaugh-lin, & Nieves, 2007) and suggests the complexity of social integration across diverse groups as reflected in the Weidman (1989) model.

Discussion

Studies published between 2003 and 2013 demonstrate that the Weidman (1989) model can contribute important insights into student identity de-velopment in college—insights that can enrich educational research and practice. Foremost among them is the recognition of the importance that the normative contexts experienced by college students can exert lasting influences on students' academic, social, and personal development. This includes the academic settings for more intellectual learning (lectures, sem-inars, laboratories, libraries, etc.), more informal settings for interaction (residence halls, fraternities and sororities, coffee shops, restaurants, etc.), and the settings in which the variety of cocurricular activities and interac-tion with faculty occur. All of these settings have the potential to contribute to student development depending on involvement and integration of the individual student.

Research using the Weidman (1989) model also illustrates the importance of normative contexts that are not necessarily under the direct control of the higher education institution, but nonetheless retain their importance for student development. Probably foremost among these normative contexts are the various settings and types of interaction with family members, from social media to home visits and vacations. While colleges have built an astonishing variety of programs focused on sharpening the normative dimensions of both cocurricular activities (often out of self-interest related to student retention) and academic activities (internships, co-operative placements, competitions, etc.), they have only recently begun establishing programs that provide continuing opportunities for linking parents to their children's undergraduate experience. This is one area in which more research using the Weidman (1989) model to study student development is needed.

Conceptualizing the undergraduate experience through the lens of the Weidman (1989) model appropriately views the campus as a set of normative contexts (academic and social) in which socialization processes (interpersonal, intrapersonal, and integration) occur and influence significant outcomes (affective and cognitive) related to student identity development. These normative environments and processes affect socialization before students enter college (anticipatory), during their collegiate experience, and well after they graduate (longer term consequences). The foregoing studies show that the Weidman model can be used flexibly and adapted for studying impacts of multiple aspects of the college experience, especially since results do not follow a singular pattern, but rather vary according to the dimensions under consideration. They also attest to its enduring utility for the study of college impact.

References

Agliata, A. K., & Renk, K. (2008). College students' adjustment: The role of parent-college student expectation discrepancies and communication reciprocity. *Journal of Youth and Adolescence, 37*(8), 967–982.

Antonio, A. L. (2004). The influence of friendship groups on intellectual self-confidence and educational aspirations in college. *Journal of Higher Education, 75*(4), 446–471.

Baxter Magolda, M. B. (2001). *Making their own way: Narratives for transforming higher education to promote self-development.* Sterling, VA: Stylus.

Bess, J. L. (Ed.). (1991). *Foundations of American higher education: An ASHE reader.* Needham Heights, MA: Ginn Press.

Bess, J. L., & Webster, D. (Eds.). (1999). *Foundations of American higher education: An ASHE reader* (2nd ed.). Needham Heights, MA: Simon & Schuster Custom Publishing.

Brim, O. G., Jr., (1966). Socialization through the life cycle. In O. G. Brim, Jr., & S. Wheeler (Eds.), *Socialization after childhood: Two essays* (pp. 1–49). New York, NY: Wiley.

Carter, D. F., Locks, A. M., & Winkle-Wagner, R. (2013). From when and where I enter: Theoretical and empirical considerations of minority students' transition to college. In M. B. Paulsen (Ed.), *Higher education: Handbook of theory and research* (Vol. 28, pp. 93–149). Dordrecht, The Netherlands: Springer.

Chickering, A. W., & Reisser, L. (1993). *Education and identity* (2nd ed.). San Francisco, CA: Jossey-Bass.

Cole, D. (2011). Debunking anti-intellectualism: An examination of African American college students' intellectual self-concepts. *Review of Higher Education, 34*(2), 259–282.

Corwin, J. R., & Cintrón, R. (2011). Social networking phenomena in the first-year experience. *Journal of College Teaching & Learning (TLC), 8*(1), 25–37.

Davis, K. E., Johnson, L., Ralston, P. A., Fields, M. E., Young-Clark, I., Colyard, V., . . . Rasco, M. R. (2010). Perceptions, experiences, and use of resources as selected HBCU students transition to graduate and professional roles in family and consumer sciences. *Family and Consumer Sciences Research Journal, 39*(1), 107–118.

Dill, B. T., McLaughlin, A. E., & Nieves, A. D. (2007). Future directions of feminist research: Intersectionality. In S. N. Hesse-Biber (Ed.), *Handbook of feminist research* (pp. 629–637). Thousand Oaks, CA: Sage.

Eagan, M. K., Hurtado, S., Chang, M. J., Garcia, G. A., Herrera, F. A., & Garibay, J. C. (2013). Making a difference in science education the impact of undergraduate research programs. *American Educational Research Journal, 50*(4), 683–713.

Engberg, M. E. (2007). Educating the workforce for the 21st century: A cross disciplinary analysis of the impact of the undergraduate experience on students' development of a pluralistic orientation. *Research in Higher Education, 48*(3), 283–317.

Espinosa, L. L. (2011). Pipelines and pathways: Women of color in undergraduate STEM majors and the college experiences that contribute to persistence. *Harvard Educational Review, 81*(2), 209–240.

Fuentes, M. V., Alvarado, A. R., Berdan, J., & DeAngelo, L. (2013). Mentorship matters: Does early faculty contact lead to quality faculty interaction? *Research in Higher Education.* Published online. doi:10.1007/s11162-013-9307-6

Holley, K. A., & Taylor, B. J. (2009). Undergraduate student socialization and learning in an online professional curriculum. *Innovative Higher Education, 33*(4), 257–269.

Inkelas, K. K. (2003). Diversity's missing minority: Asian Pacific American undergraduates' attitudes toward affirmative action. *Journal of Higher Education, 74*(6), 601–639.

Johnson, D. R. (2012). Campus racial climate perceptions and overall sense of belonging among racially diverse women in STEM majors. *Journal of College Student Development, 53*(2), 336–346.

Jones, S. R., & Abes, E. S. (2013). *Identity development of college students: Advancing frameworks for multiple dimensions of identity.* San Francisco, CA: Jossey-Bass.

Lott, J. (2013). Predictors of civic values: Understanding student-level and institutional-level effects. *Journal of College Student Development, 54*(1), 1–16.

Padgett, R. D., Goodman, K. M., Johnson, M. P., Saichaie, K., Umbach, P. D., & Pascarella, E. T. (2010). The impact of college student socialization, social class, and race on need for cognition. In S. Herzog (Ed.), *New Directions for Institutional Research: No. 145. Diversity and educational benefits* (pp. 99–111). San Francisco, CA: Jossey-Bass.

Pascarella, E. T., & Terenzini, P. T. (1991). *How college affects students.* San Francisco, CA: Jossey-Bass.

Pascarella, E. T., & Terenzini, P. T. (2005). *How college affects students, Vol. 2. A third decade of research.* San Francisco, CA: Jossey-Bass.

Sax, L. J., & Wartman, K. L. (2010). Studying the impact of parental involvement on college student development: A review and agenda for research. In J. C. Smart (Ed.),

Higher education: Handbook of theory and research (Vol. 25, pp. 219–255). Dordrecht, The Netherlands: Springer.

Spady, W. G. (1970). Dropouts from higher education: An interdisciplinary review and synthesis. *Interchange, 1*(1), 64–85.

Tinto, V. (1975). Dropout from higher education: A theoretical synthesis of recent research. *Review of Educational Research, 45*(1), 89–125.

Titus, M. A. (2004). An examination of the influence of institutional context on student persistence at 4-year colleges and universities: A multilevel approach. *Research in Higher Education, 45*(7), 673–699.

Weidman, J. C. (1984). Impacts of campus experiences and parental socialization on undergraduates' career choices. *Research in Higher Education, 20*(4), 445–476.

Weidman, J. C. (1989). Undergraduate socialization: A conceptual approach. In J. C. Smart (Ed.), *Higher education: Handbook of theory and research* (Vol. 5, pp. 289–322). New York, NY: Agathon Press.

Weidman, J. C. (2006). Socialization of students in higher education: Organizational perspectives. In C. C. Conrad & R. C. Serlin (Eds.), *The Sage handbook for research in education: Engaging ideas and enriching inquiry* (pp. 253–262). Thousand Oaks, CA: Sage.

Weidman, J. C., Twale, D. J., & Stein, E. L. (2001). Socialization of graduate and professional students in higher education: A perilous passage? *ASHE-ERIC Higher Education Report, 28*(3). San Francisco, CA: Jossey-Bass.

John C. Weidman *is a professor of higher and international development education at the University of Pittsburgh.*

Linda DeAngelo *is an assistant professor of higher education at the University of Pittsburgh.*

Kathryn A. Bethea *is a PhD student at the University of Pittsburgh.*

6

This chapter discusses how college students can develop democratic dispositions and a civic identity through learning how to engage in deliberative dialogue on public issues.

Deliberative Dialogue and the Development of Democratic Dispositions

Katy J. Harriger

Deliberative dialogue has long been seen by political theorists, particularly those interested in robust citizen engagement, as an essential component of democratic decision making, as well as an experience that can serve a positive educative function for democratic citizens. Can college students learn to be democratically engaged citizens by learning how to deliberate? This chapter will review theoretical arguments about educating for democracy, discuss experiments with deliberative dialogue on college campuses, note the promise this approach shows for the development of democratic dispositions and civic identity in college students, and propose questions for future research in this area.

Educating Democratic Citizens

Self-government requires educated citizens. This reality has long been recognized by both the enemies and friends of democracy. The enemies champion government by philosopher kings, monarchs, or elites because the masses are considered too ignorant to rule. Friends of democracy recognize the critical importance of educating citizens in order for democratic institutions to survive. Perhaps Thomas Jefferson said it most eloquently in arguing for public funds for primary and university education. In an 1820 letter he wrote, "I know no safe depository of the ultimate powers of the society, but the people themselves: and if we think them not enlightened enough to exercise their controul [*sic*] with a wholsome [*sic*] discretion, the remedy is, not to take it from them, but to inform their discretion by education" (Jefferson, 1820, para. 13). Today there is no serious dispute to the notion that democracy and education are intertwined, but the debate about what kind of education is necessary for citizens of a democracy is ongoing.

New Directions for Higher Education, no. 166, Summer 2014 © 2014 Wiley Periodicals, Inc.
Published online in Wiley Online Library (wileyonlinelibrary.com) • DOI: 10.1002/he.20095

The most traditional approach to civic education focuses on what citizens need to know about how government works and what their rights and responsibilities are as citizens of a democracy. This focus on knowledge acquisition alone has been called into question repeatedly in political science studies that demonstrate just how little American citizens know about their government (see, e.g., Bauerlein, 2008; Campbell, Converse, Miller, & Stokes, 1960; Delli Carpini & Keeter, 1996; Niemi & Junn, 1998). By these measures, traditional civic education appears to be failing to produce the kinds of citizens democracy requires.

Some democratic theorists have argued, however, that the development of citizens who understand and are committed to democratic principles and who are prepared and willing to participate in the democratic process requires more than simply learning the history and facts about one's political system. This strand of thought contends that democratic dispositions develop through practice and experience; thus, opportunities to engage in community and political activities serve an educative function that helps develop the identities of democratic citizens.

Philosopher of education John Dewey (1921) is perhaps at the forefront of this notion that citizens develop by "doing" rather than simply by "knowing," but it is a common belief among theorists of participatory democracy that it is through the opportunities to engage with others in institutions throughout the community (schools, the workplace, civic associations) that people learn the capacity for self-governance. Carole Pateman (1970) notes that democracy cannot exist simply because it has representative institutions. Instead, socialization "for democracy must take place in other spheres in order that the necessary individual attitudes and psychological qualities can be developed" (p. 42). According to Pateman, participatory theorists' answer to the elitist or antidemocratic critics is that opportunities to participate are:

> educative in the very widest sense, including both the psychological aspect and the gaining of practice in democratic skills and procedures … Participation develops and fosters the very qualities necessary for it; the more individuals participate the better able they become to do so. (pp. 42–43)

The central and interrelated questions that must first be answered in considering how to best prepare college students to live in a democracy are "What kind of democracy?" and "What kind of citizen?" If the assumption is that relatively low levels of participation are normal and desirable and that representative elites are more knowledgeable and thus better guardians of democracy (see, e.g., Dye & Zeigler, 2012), then minimal intervention is necessary through the educational process. Elites will be more educated by default, education correlates with participation and opportunities for leadership, and democracies can continue without high levels of participation by average citizens. If, on the other hand, the ideal democracy is one with high levels of engagement by a broader and more diverse group of citizens who are able and willing to engage in the political process, then a different kind of civic education is required.

Gary Biesta and Robert Lawry (2006) argue that rather than focusing on how to teach citizenship so that young people acquire knowledge about their country's political system, there ought to be more effort to understand how young people "learn democratic citizenship" (p. 64). Citing John Dewey's (1921) notion of democracy as a "mode of associated living" (p. 65), Biesta and Lawry contend that:

> "Learning democracy" comprises how young people learn about the idea of democracy and the ways it is practiced in different settings and at different levels (local, national, global); how they come to acquire the skills of deliberation and democratic decision-making; and how they come to form positive or negative dispositions towards democracy. (p. 65)

Consequently, they argue that civic education must work to "overcome the individualistic conception of citizenship that underpins much recent thinking in the area of civic education" (p. 65).

Joel Westheimer and Joseph Kahne (2004) identify three different "visions of citizenship" found in various civic education programs, each of which suggests a different civic education approach. The "personally responsible citizen" should have individual character traits that make them "honest, responsible, and law-abiding" and are best developed through character education and volunteering programs. The "participatory citizen" understands how government works and how to organize and be involved in the process in order to accomplish things with other citizens. Here civic education focuses on helping students figure out how the system operates and how to negotiate it to get things done. Finally, the "justice-oriented citizen" is one who has been taught to think critically about the existing system and learns to "question, debate, and change established systems and structures" (p. 240). It is some combination of the "participatory citizen" and the "justice-oriented citizen" that democratic theorists like Dewey (1921) and Pateman (1970) argue is necessary for democracy to thrive. To develop democratic dispositions that incline citizens toward working with others to address problems and injustice, a different kind of civic education is necessary.

This is not to argue that knowledge and cognitive skills are irrelevant to civic education, but only that alone they are not enough to ensure that citizens are democratically *engaged*. The ability to apply and put to use that knowledge in the community requires a further level of development of what John J. Patrick (2000) calls "participatory skills and civic dispositions" (p. 4). These civic dispositions include a willingness to promote "the common good of the community," to recognize "the common humanity and dignity of each person," to participate "responsibly and effectively in political and civic life," and to support and maintain "democratic principles and practices" (p. 5). Richard Battistoni (1997) has argued that education for democracy requires programs that develop "an other-regarding ethic appropriate to democratic citizenship" (p. 150).

Research on the construction of civic identities mirrors, and in some cases expands upon, the development of democratic dispositions. Both concepts take a developmental approach, but we might think of civic identity as providing the broader structure within which democratic dispositions are housed. Civic identity is defined as a "sense of connection to and participation in a civic community" (Rubin, 2007, p. 450) and "entails the establishment of individual and collective senses of social agency, responsibility for society, and political-moral awareness" (Youniss, McLellan, & Yates, 1997, p. 620). The research in this area shows that the development of civic identity occurs through practice and engagement with others and "requires active reflection, experimentation, and what Dewey called 'moral rehearsal'" (Knefelkamp, 2008, pp. 2–3).

Deliberation as an Approach to Civic Education

What kinds of civic education practices might help develop civic dispositions and identities of the sort discussed above? Attention to how to better educate students for their future roles as democratic citizens has increased significantly in the last decade. In 2012, the National Task Force on Civic Learning and Democratic Engagement released a "Call to Action" stressing the importance of taking seriously the role of higher education institutions in preparing students for civic life. The authors of the report noted that a survey of 2,400 college students in 2009 found that only a third of the respondents felt "that their civic awareness had expanded in college, that the campus had helped them learn the skills needed to effectively change society for the better, or that their commitment to improve society had grown" (p. 41). The report chronicled the many ways in which colleges and universities were responding to this call and included discussion of dialogue and deliberation as one means by which students could be taught citizenship skills and dispositions. The report noted research on the impact of deliberative dialogue projects (Association for the Study of Higher Education, 2006; Gurin, Nagda, & Sorensen, 2011; Harriger & McMillan, 2007) and concluded that the research thus far suggests deliberative dialogue is a high-impact methodology for preparing students for their civic roles (National Task Force on Civic Learning and Democratic Engagement, 2012, pp. 56–57).

Teaching students how to deliberate about issues important to their lives shows real promise in helping them develop civic dispositions and identities. Deliberative dialogue encourages participants to listen and try to understand the perspectives of people with whom they disagree and focuses on trying to find common ground for action. It involves establishing ground rules for discussion that discourage dominance by a few, storytelling to promote empathy and understanding, and surfacing the value conflicts that underlie most policy debate (Mathews & McAfee, 2002).

Experimenting With Deliberation

At Wake Forest University, my colleague Jill McMillan and I engaged in a four-year longitudinal investigation into whether learning to deliberate could have a positive impact on college students' civic engagement and attitudes about participating in the political process. In 2001, we selected a representative group of 30 students from the entering class at our university to participate in a program called Democracy Fellows. During the first semester of their first year, students took a seminar entitled "Democracy and Deliberation," which taught them both the theory and practice of deliberation. After learning about the political theory of deliberative democracy, students engaged in three deliberative dialogues about public issues, practicing their dialogue skills in the classroom setting. At the end of the seminar, the class studied their campus and learned how to frame a campus issue for a dialogue that they would be responsible for organizing and moderating. During their sophomore year, the Democracy Fellows carried out the campus dialogue. During their junior year, they organized and moderated a dialogue on the issue of urban sprawl in the Winston-Salem, North Carolina community. Finally in their senior year, they engaged in various projects at their own initiative, including moderating a regional dialogue on civic education and demonstrating their deliberative skills in a campus program on the 2004 presidential election.

At the start and end of the four years, we conducted individual interviews with each of the Democracy Fellows. In addition, after each deliberative intervention we held focus groups with the group to assess what they were learning and how the experiences were influencing the way they thought about politics and democratic engagement. Throughout the four years, we compared the Democracy Fellows to a class cohort of students who were not involved in the project. All of the students in the study filled out a participation survey annually where they identified the kinds of activities in which they were engaged. After the campus deliberation during the sophomore year, we also conducted focus groups with students who had participated in that deliberation only.

At the end of the four years, it was clear that learning to deliberate in the classroom, the campus, and the community had indeed helped the Democracy Fellows develop the democratic dispositions identified earlier. The Fellows differed from the nonparticipant cohort in several important ways. First, their notions of citizenship were far more communal or "other-regarding" than the nonparticipants. They identified the responsibilities of citizenship as requiring working with others to address the problems of society. Nonparticipants were far more likely to express an individualistic and self-interested reason for participating in politics. The Democracy Fellows, who represented majors that ranged from biology, to business, to political science, also saw politics as the work of everyone. Nonparticipants were much more likely to think that politics was what political science students did but not how they wanted to spend their time. The Fellows were also more likely to express a sense of political efficacy—the ability to have an impact on campus and in the world—than were the nonparticipants. Importantly, the Democracy Fellows also saw the way in which the skills of democratic deliberation were useful well beyond the political sphere. They talked about how the practices of deliberation were applicable in their everyday lives: listening carefully to others, hearing and telling stories, asking who is not at the table and what might they say, identifying the value conflicts that underlie disagreement, and weighing the tradeoffs involved in policy choice. They were using these skills in their other classes, in their organizations, and in their relationships with roommates, friends, and family.

Four years of deliberative experience had an impact on the Democracy Fellows. What was equally interesting, however, was that substantially smaller interventions also appeared to have a positive impact. The students from across campus who participated in the on-campus deliberation were uniformly positive and excited about the experience, recognizing how different it was from the ways in which they usually talked about issues. We concluded our study by suggesting that there were myriad places on college campuses where deliberative dialogue could be taught and practiced, including the classroom, residence halls, and student organizations (Harriger & McMillan, 2007).

Experiments with deliberation are happening across the country in higher education institutions both large and small. Writing classes at Michigan State University and first-year seminars at Franklin Pierce College in New Hampshire have used deliberative dialogue as a means of connecting students with the larger community and teaching them to think and write critically about public issues. Deliberative dialogue has been used in teacher-training programs and as a way to get Greek organizations to take seriously their espoused fraternal values (Dedrick, Grattan, & Dienstfrey, 2008). The impact of deliberation on attitudes and behavior has been studied now in multiple contexts, including not just the classroom and higher education (Dedrick et al., 2008; Harriger & McMillan, 2007; London, 2010) but also in communities in the United States and across the world (see, e.g., Nabatchi, 2010; Nabatchi, Gastil, Weiksner, & Leighninger, 2012; Niemeyer, 2011). The degree to which interest has grown in this approach as a way of addressing the "democratic deficit" (Nabatchi, 2010) is reflected in the fact that the *Annual Review of Political Science* included an extensive review essay in 2004 on the research into deliberation (Delli Carpini, Cook, & Jacobs, 2004) and what we know and do not know about its impact on civic attitudes and behavior.

The Need for Further Research

An additional measure of the amount of attention being paid to the impact of civic education practices is the current focus on the need to assess what we know and what we still need to learn about what works to create "long-lasting habits of civic engagement" (Hollander & Burack, 2009). In 2008, The Spencer Foundation, which focuses its philanthropic efforts on supporting educational research, brought together a group of scholars and practitioners in the area of civic engagement to discuss the state of the field. Their conclusions about the research agenda going forward included (a) the need to identify "the academic and cocurricular elements that most impact student civic engagement and long-term commitment to civic engagement," and (b) the need for longitudinal approaches and data (Hollander & Burack, 2009, pp. 6–8).

Peter Levine (2011) notes that "the application of deliberative democracy to youth civic engagement has not been thoroughly explored, but the clear implication is that young people should learn to deliberate" (p. 17). At the end of four years, our Democracy Fellows had developed democratic dispositions that were different from their fellow students who did not participate in the process. Beyond our own 2007 study, reviews of the literature suggest that the experience of deliberating has a positive impact on developing civic skills (Hess, 2009). Certainly, more studies across different campuses would be important in trying to replicate our findings. It would also be important to understand what aspects of the deliberative experience have the most impact on shaping democratic dispositions and civic identities. Beyond that, as the Spencer Foundation study suggested, there is a need to know whether the impact measured while students are still in college is sustained over time when students enter "the real world." What is the impact of a national polarized politics on willingness to engage with others? Do democratic dispositions stick, or are they lost to disillusionment with politics as usual? How enduring are the civic identities developed in college? How do the experiences of the workplace shape attitudes about civic engagement?

The participatory theorists discussed at the start of this essay share the notion that democratic dispositions are learned through experience. As Biesta and Lawry (2006) remind us, however, antidemocratic dispositions are learned as well. Civic identities may be as attached to maintenance of the status quo as they are to working for social change (Youniss et al., 1997, p. 630). We can teach democratic theory all day long, but if what students (and alumni) are encountering in the other spaces in their lives are unequal and authoritarian institutions and practices, the likelihood that they will *believe* in and *live* that theory is diminished. Undemocratic experiences may in fact create very weak civic identities where students' lack of a sense of agency stands in the way of their being able to participate effectively in a deliberation or take advantage of civic engagement opportunities that are available. As higher education faculty and staff, we need to know much more about whether and how democratic dispositions and civic identities can be developed and sustained in the face of undemocratic experiences.

References

Association for the Study of Higher Education (ASHE). (2006). Research on outcomes and processes of inter-group dialogue. *Higher Education Report*, *32*(4), 59–73.

Battistoni, R. (1997). Service learning and democratic citizenship. *Theory into Practice*, *36*(3), 150–156.

Bauerlein, M. (2008). *The dumbest generation: How the digital age stupefies young Americans and jeopardizes our future, or don't trust anyone under 30*. New York, NY: Penguin.

Biesta, G., & Lawry, R. (2006). From teaching citizenship to learning democracy: Overcoming individualism in research, policy and practice. *Cambridge Journal of Education*, *36*(1), 63–79.

Campbell, A., Converse, P., Miller, W., & Stokes, D. (1960). *The American voter*. New York, NY: Wiley.

Dedrick, J., Grattan, L., & Dienstfrey, H. (Eds.). (2008). *Deliberation and the work of higher education: Innovations for the classroom, the campus, and the community*. Dayton, OH: Kettering Foundation Press.

Delli Carpini, M., Cook, F., & Jacobs, L. (2004). Public deliberation, discursive participation, and citizen engagement. *Annual Review of Political Science*, *7*, 315–344.

Delli Carpini, M., & Keeter, S. (1996). *What Americans know about politics and why it matters*. New Haven, CT: Yale University Press.

Dewey, J. (1921). *Democracy and education*. New York, NY: Macmillan.

Dye, T., & Zeigler, H. (2012). *The irony of democracy: An uncommon introduction to American politics*. Fort Worth, TX: Harcourt Brace.

Gurin, P., Nagda, B., & Sorensen, N. (2011). Intergroup dialogue: Education for a broad conception of civic engagement. *Liberal Education*, *97*(2), 46–51.

Harriger, K., & McMillan, J. (2007). *Speaking of politics: Preparing college students for democratic citizenship through deliberative dialogue*. Dayton, OH: Kettering Foundation Press.

Hess, D. E. (2009). *Controversy in the classroom: The democratic power of discussion*. New York, NY: Routledge.

Hollander, E., & Burack, C. (2009). *How young people develop long-lasting habits of civic engagement: A conversation on building a research agenda*. Retrieved from http://www.compact.org/wp-content/uploads/2009/05/spencerconversationre searchagenda1.pdf

Jefferson, T. (1820). To William C. Jarvis. *Quotations on education*. Retrieved from http://www.monticello.org/site/jefferson/quotations-education

Knefelkamp, L. L. (2008). Civic identity: Locating self in community. *Diversity and Democracy*, *11*(2), 1–3.

Levine, P. (2011). What do we know about civic engagement? *Liberal Education*, *97*(2), 12–19.

London, S. (2010). *Doing democracy: How a network of grass roots organizations is strengthening community, building capacity, and shaping a new kind of civic education*. Dayton, OH: Kettering Foundation Press.

Mathews, D., & McAfee, N. (2002). *Making choices together: The power of public deliberation*. Dayton, OH: Kettering Foundation Press.

Nabatchi, T. (2010). Addressing the citizenship and democratic deficits: Exploring the potential of deliberative democracy for public administration. *American Review of Public Administration*, *40*(4), 376–399.

Nabatchi, T., Gastil, J., Weiksner, M., & Leighninger, M. (Eds.). (2012). *Democracy in motion: Evaluating the practice and impact of deliberative civic engagement.* New York, NY: Oxford University Press.

National Task Force on Civic Learning and Democratic Engagement. (2012). *A crucible moment: College learning and democracy's future.* Washington, DC: Association of American Colleges and Universities (AAC&U).

Niemeyer, S. (2011). The emancipatory effect of deliberation: Empirical lessons from mini-publics. *Politics and Society, 39*(1), 103–140.

Niemi, R., & Junn, J. (1998). *Civic education: What makes students learn.* New Haven, CT: Yale University Press.

Pateman, C. (1970). *Participation and democratic theory.* Cambridge, England: Cambridge University Press.

Patrick, J. (2000). Introduction to education for civic engagement in democracy. In S. Mann & J. Patrick (Eds.), *Education for civic engagement in democracy: Service learning and other promising practices* (pp. 1–8). Bloomington, IN: ERIC.

Rubin, B. (2007). "There's still not justice": Youth civic identity development amid distinct school and community contexts. *Teachers College Record, 109*(2), 449–481.

Westheimer, J., & Kahne, J. (2004). What kind of citizen? The politics of educating for democracy. *American Educational Research Journal, 41*(2), 237–269.

Youniss, J., McLellan, J. A., & Yates, M. (1997). What we know about engendering civic identity. *The American Behavioral Scientist, 40*(5), 620–631.

KATY J. HARRIGER is a professor and the chair of the Department of Politics and International Affairs at Wake Forest University.

7

This chapter provides guidelines and suggestions for assessing student development using autoethnography, a qualitative research method. Autoethnography guides students in examining the nexus between personal and professional identities, including skills, challenges, values, histories, and hopes for the future.

Autoethnography: Inquiry Into Identity

Steve Hoppes

I am confused. I am confused by the sheer irrationality, ambiguity, and abundance of things coming into being at all. I am confused by having been born into a world from which I will be ejected at death. I am confused as to who or why I am. I am confused by the labyrinth of choices I face. I don't know what to do.

(Batchelor, 1997, p. 67)

As meaning-seeking beings, we face rich opportunities and perplexing conundrums in understanding identity. We yearn to understand who we are, what we are doing, why we are doing it, and what the future holds. We face questions, such as the following:

- What is this life about?
- Who exactly am I in this moment?
- What are my personal and professional paths really about, how are they related, and where are they taking me?
- Am I prepared for the challenges ahead?

These puzzles can be particularly nettling for traditional-age college students who tend to be long on hopes and ideals but short on life experience and perspective.

As students move from college classrooms, where they enter neat and tidy "answers" onto exams based on studied facts and theories, into the messy world that lies beyond, they often find that their ready-made "answers" are surprisingly flimsy. As students begin the long climb up a career ladder, it may dawn on them that they have no idea who they are, what is going on, why they are here, or where they are headed. As they

New Directions for Higher Education, no. 166, Summer 2014 © 2014 Wiley Periodicals, Inc.
Published online in Wiley Online Library (wileyonlinelibrary.com) • DOI: 10.1002/he.20096

scramble to make sense of it, their primary motive may be to keep from appearing stupid. In time, all of us tend to adapt to the challenges we face, more or less, making many mistakes along the way. Our existential questions-without-answers may periodically go dormant beneath the surface of our busy lives but can resurface at any time. We gradually realize that we will never fully understand. Even so, that does not stop us from probing. Stress, loss, and change—never far away—revitalize our questions. Although inquiry cannot yield solid, static answers to life's mysteries, it has the power to heal minds and hearts. I routinely saw this happen in a course I taught on autoethnography.

What Is Autoethnography?

Hayano (1979) coined the term "autoethnography" to describe ethnographic research done on one's "own people" through an insider's perspective (p. 99). Reed-Danahay (1997) broadened the definition of autoethnography to include "autobiographical writing that has ethnographic interest" (p. 2). Autoethnography has been called a "postmodern form of ethnography" (Neville-Jan, 2003, p. 89) and "an autobiographical genre of writing and research that displays multiple layers of consciousness, connecting the personal to the cultural" (Ellis & Bochner, 2000, p. 739).

Autoethnographers' methods vary, but generally include discussion, reflection, note-taking, emotional recall, and identification of categories and themes yielding a narrative that affords both the inside view of a research participant and the outside view of a researcher (Ellis, 1998; Ellis & Bochner, 2000). A small sampling demonstrates the range of autoethnographers' research interests: living with chronic pain caused by spina bifida (Neville-Jan, 2003, 2005), the impact of death on families (Ellis, 1993; Hoppes, 2005a), meanings and purposes of care-giving for a family member (Hoppes, 2005b; Salmon, 2006; Thibeault, 1997), a family's journey through perinatal loss (Forhan, 2010), growing up with a parent with mental retardation (Ronai, 1996), and an insider's perspective on bulimia (Tillmann-Healy, 1996). By placing the writer in dual roles of researcher and research participant, autoethnography is a meaning-making tool that facilitates the exploration of identity.

Designing a Course Based on Autoethnography

In client-centered professions, learning about oneself and one's interpersonal skills and challenges is intrinsic to professional development. Autoethnography, a blend of qualitative research methods and self-reflection, is a precise tool for those purposes. The examples that follow come from an experience with autoethnography in the curriculum of one client-centered profession. I believe that autoethnography is a flexible tool that can be applied to any number of curricula and professions.

Several years ago, my colleagues and I wanted to help our occupational therapy students on the threshold of graduation understand their changing identities. Our students face many high-stakes challenges during the three years they spend with us. After a highly selective admissions process, the rigors of the curriculum include cadaver anatomy, neuroanatomy, pediatrics, biomechanics, mental health, and several clinical rotations. Standards to pass courses are high. In the clinic, students work with clients and families experiencing autism, dementia, stroke, Parkinson's disease, spinal cord injuries, etc. Of course, students' personal lives do not stand still during this time as they navigate psychosocial stages typically marked by identity and role confusion as well as problems of intimacy and isolation (Erikson, 1959).

Reading and writing autoethnographies became the heart of our curriculum's capstone course. Here, students found a place to survey rapidly changing internal and external landscapes, including their hopes, dreams, fears, and questions about their unknowable futures. In this course, students have skillfully analyzed and documented their emerging professional and personal identities.

Our students' autoethnographies examine experiences during clinical fieldwork as a starting point. They begin by addressing a series of questions: What professional and personal strengths and weaknesses did they bring to these experiences? What challenges arose? What did they learn about themselves and their clients? What does it mean to be an occupational therapist? What did they hope for when they decided to become occupational therapists, and were these hopes dashed, realized, or transformed? How have their personal histories influenced the occupational therapist they are becoming?

Course Logistics

The first step in designing a class that makes use of autoethnography is to fit the course carefully to the environment, students, and goals. Because these variables are unique to each setting, in lieu of detailed logistics I offer a few general suggestions based on my experience.

After a short overview of the format and purpose of autoethnography, we break into small, weekly discussion groups of five to ten students led by a faculty facilitator. During the first several weeks, we assign outstanding examples of autoethnography for students to read and discuss. These models help students consider how they wish to shape their manuscripts. Those who are unfamiliar with autoethnographic literature might begin with the references cited in this chapter. Additional searches for autoethnographies for class discussions might continue with the work of Carolyn Ellis (1997, 1998) who has done more than anyone to legitimize autoethnography as a rigorous form of qualitative research. Ellis's autoethnographies are deep, self-reflective, page-turners. Her students have also made significant contributions to autoethnographic literature.

During the first few classes, students tell stories about something that happened during fieldwork. The instructor sits, listens, and sparingly asks questions. If fieldwork is not part of the academic program, instructors could ask students to tell stories about why they chose to enter their profession, early personal and professional influences and mentors, and their hopes and dreams for their careers. Once students understand that their stories will be the heart of their autoethnographies, their semester's work is set in motion.

In subsequent weeks, students share drafts of their developing autoethnographies prior to group meetings for peer review and subsequent discussion. Classmates, who by this time in our program tend to be tightly bonded, draw on their close relationships to offer valuable advice and to help each other define what is important in their stories and reflections.

Finding a Story to Tell and Defining a Research Question

Some students know immediately the stories they wish to tell in their autoethnographies; some initially struggle to find stories or choose the "right one." We ask uncertain students, "Is it possible that, instead of choosing a story to tell, your story will choose you?" Students may find this question as inscrutable as a Zen koan, but we mean to suggest that, at crucial junctures in our lives, we each have stories that must be told because of their instructive potentials to guide us. We have found that meaningful stories and students who are ready to learn from them tend to find each other in the process of group discussions, coupled with writing and rewriting. As a result, autoethnography becomes a powerful medium for reflection and the expression of identity.

We emphasize that autoethnography, like other forms of research, hinges on a well-articulated research question, although it very likely will be implicit instead of explicit. Throughout the writing and reviewing process, we ask students, again and again, to think about the importance of their stories and themes in light of research questions that their autoethnographies might address. Often, the research question may not be evident to the writer and is one of the last puzzle pieces to fall into place. Our students' autoethnographies have addressed research questions such as: How does an occupational therapist define boundaries between personal and professional lives? How does an occupational therapist learn to deal with loss? And, how does adversity in an occupational therapist's personal life influence empathy and understanding of clients? Classmates and the instructor will often infer the research questions from discussions and reading early drafts before the author can articulate them.

Moving Around in a Story

Autoethnography "fluently moves back and forth, first looking inward, then outward, then backward, and forward, until the distinctions between the individual and social are blurred beyond recognition and the past, present, and future become continuous" (Ellis, 1997, pp. 132–133). Often, students are not sure why certain clinical events, such as the death of a favorite patient or working with a child with severe disabilities, hit them with such force. In telling these stories, students can become "stuck," unsure of what the story means, personally and professionally. At this point, the facilitator can best serve students by asking a few gentle questions to help them *move around* in their stories: Why was this patient special to you? Did she remind you of someone else in your life? What do you think you meant to her, and what did she mean to you? What would an objective observer say about your interaction with this patient and her family? What would someone who knows you well say? How did your past inform your work with her and her family? What did you learn from this experience that you will carry forward?

These questions help authors become unstuck in time and perspective. By considering viewpoints of clients, families, and peers, and by recalling the past and imagining the future, they begin to awaken to generative forces that shaped personal and professional responses. Autoethnography's "inward–outward/backward–forward" storytelling method shines light on meanings that, ordinarily, are not available.

As excerpts from the following autoethnography illustrate, these revealed meanings form the foundations for clearer understandings of changing identity. While space allows for analysis of only one student's autoethnography (used with permission and pseudonyms), this depth of reflection and analysis tends to be the norm for students that I have worked with over the years. All of my students have used autoethnography to peel back at least a layer or two; many go much deeper. Students seem to know what they are ready to become aware of. I have found that autoethnography, skillfully presented, has almost universal appeal to students.

Unlocking the Past to Open the Future

> The past is never dead. It's not even past.
> William Faulkner (1951, p. 80)

Jami returned from fieldwork burdened with sadness and confusion. She did her best to put a brave face on things so she could finish coursework, graduate, and get on with her career.

At the outset of the autoethnography course, we suggested to Jami and her classmates that a story might "choose" them. Jami thought this was preposterous. In the preface of her autoethnography she wrote:

> Okay, I have to tell a story about me, but what story do I tell? My professors were quick to clear this up for me. They stated that I will not choose my

story; my story will choose me. Okay, whatever! I am the one who has to decide what to write about so obviously I will be choosing the story. Right? I was completely wrong on this issue.

Jami's autoethnography told the story of her relationship with Big Mike, an oppositional, angry patient with a lethal mix of chronic obstructive pulmonary disease, dementia, and lung cancer. During her work with Big Mike, she was surprised to find that:

> I truly cared about this man, not only as a patient but as a person, and that he cared about me. Our relationship continued to strengthen as our time together increased. His wife also noticed that we had a special bond, and she thanked me for giving so much of myself to him.

During Jami's fieldwork, Mike died suddenly, affecting her deeply. Upon learning that Mike had died, she processed the loss with her fieldwork supervisor:

> She came over and gave me a hug trying hard to console me. I didn't want the hug but I knew I needed it. "You okay?" She asked as she wiped away a tear from my cheek. "I'll be okay, it just hurts," I said as I gave her another hug, trying to just forget about it all. *I just want to forget about it and move on. He's in a better place now and I need to move on and help my other patients.*

Jami found that forgetting and moving on were not in the cards. She wrote:

> The more I sat around trying to decide what to write about, the more a particular story came to the forefront of my mind. No matter what I did to try to clear my thoughts, my mind seemed to always go back to it. I felt like I had to get this story out and let everyone know what I had gone through. I needed to release myself from the emotions of this story and this autoethnography was just the outlet that I needed.

Before she could move on, Jami needed to understand her attachment to Mike, which involved a side-trip to her past. As an instructor, my work is to help students move around in their stories by asking the right questions at the right times. Jami wrote:

> Why this patient? I've worked with so many patients over the two and a half years I've been in this program, what made him so special? Why did I get so upset? Why Mike? For the longest time I never knew the answer to that question and it kept burning a hole in me. I was unable to come up with an answer until I started writing this autoethnography. My professor point-blank asked me why this story hit me so hard. Without even thinking I blurted

out, "Because he reminds me of my granddad." My answer shocked me and I couldn't believe what I had said.

Jami went on to recount the death of her grandfather and her inability to grieve his loss satisfactorily at the time. How has my history shaped who I am? Who am I in this moment? What does my future hold? This is how Jami answered those questions to conclude her autoethnography:

> I believe Mike was sent to me to help me deal with unresolved emotions and to open my eyes to a side I never really knew existed. I have a responsibility to my patients to help them get better, but I also, when called upon, have a responsibility to help make their transitions into death easier and more comfortable. *I did not bargain for this. I want to help people live, not die!* It may not be something I *want* to do, but I have a responsibility to my patients. We as occupational therapists have a responsibility to our patients, and sometimes death is part of those responsibilities. Learning this lesson as a student was very difficult. I have learned what my responsibilities are and that I am strong enough to handle them.

Leaning Into Life's Sharp Points

Inquiries into loss and broken-heartedness are necessary steps on the path of understanding who we are. I have seen this with my students and I have seen this with myself. Buddhist teachers instruct that leaning into life's sharp points yields life's greatest lessons. Pema Chodron (2000) expressed it this way:

> The trick is to keep exploring and not bail out, even when we find out that something is not what we thought. That's what we're going to discover again and again and again. Nothing is what we thought. I can say that with great confidence. Emptiness is not what we thought. Neither is mindfulness or fear. Compassion—not what we thought. Love. Buddha nature. Courage. These are code words for things we don't know in our minds, but any of us could experience them. These are words that point to what life really is when we let things fall apart and let ourselves be nailed to the present moment. (p. 5)

We might add the term "identity" to the list of constructs that are not what we thought but point to what life really is when things fall apart and we come into the present. Autoethnography illuminates this process. Jami had unspoken, painful questions that she couldn't articulate or answer: Why do I hurt so much? How can I find peace? How do I move forward? Is that even possible? As humans, we are hard-wired to find pain aversive, and when it is thrust upon us, as it was for Jami, we generally fight it, try to fix it, or flee from it. In the long run, none of these strategies bring relief; only one pathway heals pain: the one that goes straight through it.

Autoethnography guided Jami through her pain. By carefully and persistently moving around in her story—going inward and outward, forward and back—she was able to let things fall apart, come into the present to peel back emotional layers, and articulate strengths she did not know that she possessed. By understanding her pain, she acknowledged that she found peace and a way forward, marked by acceptance, awareness, and self-compassion.

Conclusion

Autoethnography is a kind of meditation that teaches us to sit comfortably with questions that have no answers and to meet ourselves with kindness and understanding, even when we are hurting, anxious, or afraid. Autoethnographers are invited to meet and accept their lives in all of their messiness, joy, and sorrow.

Autoethnography facilitates students' inquiry into their confusing and challenging lives without hope of finding rational, solid, static answers, but with trust that it will settle and heal their hearts, even if that means first breaking them wide open to discover their humanness. Autoethnography helps us see that everything changes and that identity is something one lives, not something one has.

As educators, we may not know how to write and actualize learning objectives that address the complexities of pain, awareness, self-compassion, and identity. Autoethnography opens these doors and students can walk through them at their own pace when they are ready.

References

Batchelor, S. (1997). *Buddhism without beliefs*. New York, NY: Riverhead Books.

Chodron, P. (2000). *When things fall apart: Heart advice for difficult times*. Boston, MA: Shambhala.

Ellis, C. (1993). There are survivors: Telling a story of sudden death. *Sociological Quarterly, 34*(4), 711–730.

Ellis, C. (1997). Evocative autoethnography: Writing emotionally about our lives. In W. Tierney & Y. Lincoln (Eds.), *Representation and the text: Re-framing the narrative voice* (pp. 115–142). New York: State University of New York Press.

Ellis, C. (1998). Exploring loss through autoethnographic inquiry: Autoethnographic stories, co-constructed narratives, and interactive interviews. In J. Harvey (Ed.), *Perspectives on loss: A sourcebook* (pp. 49–62). Philadelphia, PA: Brunner/Mazel.

Ellis, C., & Bochner, A. (2000). Autoethnography, personal narrative, reflexivity: Research as subject. In N. K. Denzin & Y. S. Lincoln (Eds.), *Handbook of qualitative research* (2nd ed., pp. 733–769). Thousand Oaks, CA: Sage.

Erikson, E. H. (1959). *Identity and the life cycle*. New York, NY: International Universities Press.

Faulkner, W. (1951). *Requiem for a nun*. New York, NY: Random House.

Forhan, M. (2010). Doing, being, and becoming: A family's journey through perinatal loss. *American Journal of Occupational Therapy, 64*(1), 142–151.

Hayano, D. (1979). Auto-ethnography: Paradigms, problems, and prospects. *Human Organization, 38*, 99–104.

Hoppes, S. (2005a). When a child dies the world should stop spinning: An autoethnography exploring the impact of family loss on occupation. *American Journal of Occupational Therapy, 59*(1), 78–87.

Hoppes, S. (2005b). Meanings and purposes of family caregiving: An autoethnography. *American Journal of Occupational Therapy, 59*(3), 262–272.

Neville-Jan, A. (2003). Encounters in a world of pain: An autoethnography. *American Journal of Occupational Therapy, 57*(1), 88–98.

Neville-Jan, A. (2005). The problem with prevention: The case of spina bifida. *American Journal of Occupational Therapy, 59*(5), 527–539.

Reed-Danahay, D. (1997). Introduction. In D. Reed-Danahay (Ed.), *Auto/Ethnography: Rewriting the self and the social* (pp. 1–17). New York, NY: Berg.

Ronai, C. R. (1996). My mother is mentally retarded. In C. Ellis & A. Bochner (Eds.), *Composing ethnography: Alternative forms of qualitative writing* (pp. 109–131). Walnut Creek, CA: Alta Mira Press.

Salmon, N. (2006). The waiting place: A caregiver's narrative. *Australian Occupational Therapy Journal, 53*(3), 181–187.

Thibeault, R. (1997). A funeral for my father's mind: A therapist's attempt at grieving. *Canadian Journal of Occupational Therapy, 64*(3), 107–114.

Tillmann-Healy, L. M. (1996). A secret life in a culture of thinness: Reflections on body, food, and bulimia. In C. Ellis & A. Bochner (Eds.), *Composing ethnography: Alternative forms of qualitative writing* (pp. 76–108). Walnut Creek, CA: Alta Mira Press.

STEVE HOPPES *teaches mindfulness in Tulsa, Oklahoma.*

.

8

This chapter describes a pedagogy for enlisting international diversity on campus to "shake up" understanding of self and other in a half Asian/half American international classroom. Results from the practice are presented, along with suggestions for future adaptations in a range of settings.

Shaking It Up: Deconstructing Self and Other in an International Classroom

Cathy A. Small

In the spring of 2002, out of a lingering frustration with my life and role as a professor, I applied to my own university as a freshman. I did so out of the belief that taking classes for a year and leaving my home environment for a "dorm" (now, I learned, called residence hall) would invoke the empathy and insight for my students that often comes with walking in another's shoes.

The experience, which I recounted in *My Freshman Year* (Nathan, 2005), was transformative for me. It resulted in my renewed energy as a professor as well as a decade-long quest to respond in my pedagogy and curriculum to my new understandings about students, undergraduate culture, and university education. One of the salient questions I had in returning to the classroom was how to foster or invoke in my classes the deep "liminal" potential of the university experience to transform ourselves and worldviews.

What I describe in this chapter is one such response, focused on global understanding—one of the three new courses I first piloted and then submitted for adoption as part of the liberal studies curriculum at Northern Arizona University. The course was supported by the Center for International Education, whose advising support made the logistics of this half international and half U.S. course possible.

"Connecting across Cultures," as students ultimately named it, is an introductory anthropology course specifically designed to encourage different cultural groups to interact and, through this interaction, to explore course content, which includes standard cultural anthropology topics, such as: family and kinship, wealth and exchange, religion and worldview, beauty

New Directions for Higher Education, no. 166, Summer 2014 © 2014 Wiley Periodicals, Inc.
Published online in Wiley Online Library (wileyonlinelibrary.com) • DOI: 10.1002/he.20097

and health, self and community. Its inception and development was guided by two insights from *My Freshman Year* (Nathan, 2005).

First was the startling separation of academic and personal life. The problem was *not*, as I had once suspected, that college no longer spurs the deep liminal experiences that transform worldview and self-definition; it was rather that the deepest and most transformative learning experiences were *not* primarily happening in the classroom. Many student colleagues reported to me that they rarely remember course content (no less the professor's name) a semester after they completed a course, even though they earned an A. I asked them, "Would you say you came to college to learn?" "Most definitely!" was the response. In fact, almost 80% of students in my anonymous survey indicated that, if given the chance to simply pay for their credits and leave with a degree, they would stay in school. But their reasons for doing so were more about "the college experience" than their classes; when asked directly how much of their learning occurred outside versus inside their classes, the median response was 65% outside and 35% inside. There was little social glue to connect their academic and personal lives. I was surprised to learn that students' social networks had little to do with shared academic interests, and few students met their closest friends through classes (Nathan, 2005).

My second insight concerned the way in which social homogeneity was limiting the transformative power of the university experience. As a professor, I took heart in the growing ethnic, racial, and international diversity of our universities and the natural opportunities for learning these presented both in and out of the classroom. What I noticed as a student, however, was how little university diversity translated into daily social interactions, friendships, or even diverse dining partners. From interviews with students, I found that the two to six people who made up students' close personal networks were surprisingly enduring from their freshman to senior years and, especially for White students, drew on people from similar racial, ethnic, and national backgrounds. International students, who were active and visible during our preclass social, seminar, and sports activities, wound up in enclaves of other international students within one month of the semester's start. For most students, the potential of diversity to illuminate or "shake up" their own perspectives was untapped (Nathan, 2005).

The Course and the Pedagogy

What I set out to do was construct an introductory-level anthropology course that engaged students intimately and meaningfully with students from different cultural/national backgrounds. Through these encounters, I aimed to both increase their knowledge and appreciation of other cultural life ways and engage students in a critical dive into their own personal and cultural identities, one that would meld academic and personal spheres.

New Directions for Higher Education • DOI: 10.1002/he

On the first day of class, composed of half U.S., one-quarter Korean, and one-quarter Chinese students, I suggested that we all possess a largely invisible (to ourselves) cultural mask that colors both how we understand the world, ourselves, and others. To see another, we must see ourselves and vice versa, because the questions of "Who are You?" and "Who am I?" are mutually entwined, and what is more, the boundaries that these questions create are themselves suspect.

The course presents self and identity as cultural constructions to be noticed, examined, and penetrated. Unlike academic approaches that encourage students to define themselves more solidly and distinctly—by determining their beliefs, defending their opinions, and voicing their preferences—this course invites students to loosen identification with concepts of who we are. Its goal is to shake up identity by loosening its supports, exposing the unsteady foundation on which our opinions and beliefs rest. The process can be disconcerting, but it is also playful and exciting, opening the way for new intercultural understandings and encounters.

For a 15-week course, this is not an easy undertaking. It can be a life-long challenge to view all that we have come to believe and be without attachment and judgment; encounters with difference do not automatically result in understanding and empathy. Allport's (1954/1979) groundbreaking research on prejudice from the 1950s, in fact, showed that contact with racial difference, both among Blacks and Whites, was just as likely to increase stereotypes and prejudice as mitigate them. Those whose interracial contact increased their openness and friendliness for racial difference were not "special" people; rather they had "special" encounters, specifically interactions with the other that were structured in more equal and intimate ways. Sharing common goals, as in membership on an athletic team or army unit, and having mutual experiences of greater personal depth, such as a shared victory or a harrowing battle, cut through prejudice whereas encounters rooted in hierarchy (supervisor/worker, employee/employer, officer/enlisted) and in superficial mundane interactions tended to solidify and augment prejudice. Structuring the cross-cultural encounters for the class, therefore, became a central concern of the pedagogy. The course enlisted three intersecting pedagogical strategies to accomplish its aims:

1. *Cross-cultural interaction and intimacy.* Students were confronted weekly with different cultural approaches to problems, beliefs, and interactions from around the world that differed from their own. Although cross-cultural readings and lectures were solidly part of the course format, students spent time every class in small group and larger group interaction that encouraged a deeper-than-academic level of exchange. An experiential pedagogy was emphasized where the class "encountered" the differences—participating in a Korean student skit of a typical class or a bidding competition with class-issued money for a value (such as "professional recognition" or

"family harmony") in a values auction where students competitively bid to "win" 20 different cultural values. The auction was a visceral and engaged way for students to see where they, individually or culturally, put their priorities. There are myriad auction protocols available on the Internet that contain value descriptions and auction score sheets. For this class, I pieced together an auction protocol that included both classic Western values and Confucian values such as "Harmony" and "Good Reputation."

Out-of-class weekly assignments typically involved a structured interaction with a cross-cultural partner that blurred the line of personal and academic: meeting a partner's parent or family member on Skype and learning to introduce oneself appropriately, going on each other's social network page, and cooking and sharing a meal in the tradition of one's family. The two longest written assignments for the course consisted of two different structured interviews with cross-cultural partners in which intimate, personal topics are broached: from fears and challenges in childhood and the dynamics of family life, to what happens after death; from what is a successful life or what is beautiful, to which products they use on their bodies.

2. *Reflexivity*. Reflection was key to the success of the first strategy, and indeed the entire class. Reflexive inquiry asks students to use their reactions and opinions regarding cross-cultural content as a mirror that reflects back information about themselves. It is a technique that continuously redirects judgments, characterizations, and reactions about "the other" back to self-inquiry.

Imagine the first week of class where a clip of a 1980s Chinese preschool[1] includes a scene about "bathroom time" (Tobin, Hsueh, & Karasawa, 2011). An entire class of four- to five-year-old girls and boys are led into an open room with two concrete parallel troughs running down the perimeters of the room. Children pull down their pants and squat, in two rows, go to the bathroom in tandem, and then all file out to wash their hands.

I ask students to employ three questions, posed by Sunstein and Chiseri-Strater (2011) in their book *Fieldworking* as a basis for exploring personal reactions to cross-cultural content: "What disturbs me? Intrigues me? Surprises me?" (p. 87). Routinely, the bathroom footage triggers strong reactions from U.S. and Korean students who find the scene disturbingly unacceptable.

"But what exactly is disturbing?" I question. Many answers return: "The boys and girls can see each other; there are no doors; no toilets—it's a health hazard; children must all go to the bathroom together." I ask, "And why is this so disturbing? What in your own cultural schema is violated? What assumptions underlie your problem with this?" The "taken for granted" is continually probed in this way so that in place of judging 1980s Chinese child-rearing approaches, students end up investigating their own connections to individual-ism and autonomy, views of children and sexuality, privacy, cleanli-ness, and/or health. Students may not always arrive at a clear answer about their own culture but it is a very different inquiry that they pose. Weekly papers called for a similar process of self-questioning, and students vastly improved in their abilities to reflexively explore their reactions and "see themselves" as the semester progressed.

A reflexive technique was encouraged not only in academic matters—such as reactions to a reading or film—but also in inter-personal encounters including disagreements or misconnections with partners: My partner isn't on time ... my partner spends so much time telling me about himself, and so forth. In this way, difficult encoun-ters provided fodder for exploration and self-knowledge, rather than solidifying into stereotypes and prejudice.

3. *Shifting the boundaries of "us" and "them."* In a sense, we used one form of group identification to question and "rock" the ground of another. Although groups of the same nationality worked together in class on certain issues, many experiential exercises in and out of class involved conscious attempts to reposition or blur national identification. Our prepared competitive debate about the advantages of arranged ver-sus "love" marriage specified a set number of spots for U.S., Chinese, and Korean students on each side so that one's "team" evenly cross-cut national boundaries. For certain assignments, cross-cultural part-ners might be required to complete a joint analysis for a single grade; some class activities joined same-sex members of different cultures while others, like the values auction, pointed out the variation within national groups.

One seminal activity in this process is called "BaFaBaFa," a com-mercially available educational and cultural simulation game (http://www.stsintl.com/business/bafa.html), in which, early in the semester, half of the Koreans, Chinese, and U.S. students are assigned to Alpha culture and the other half to Beta culture. Students learn their assigned culture, which has distinct rules and interactional patterns (one culture even has its own language). Alpha and Beta members then perform their respective cultures, send emissaries to the other culture in order to figure out its rules, and return to their home culture with information. The simulation not only plays like an ethnographic detective game but it also gives students valuable experience in cross-cultural interaction.

Visiting the other culture often feels alienating and confusing. Its peo-ple seem mean, inscrutable, or unfriendly. The visitors, conversely, seem clueless, rude, or clumsy. Pejorative adjectives about the "other" fly freely, while Alphans come to feel warmly toward other Alphans and Betans all say that, if given a choice, they would rather be a Betan. A Korean student wrote, "This is the first time since coming to this country that I felt like

I belonged. I LOVE my Alpha culture classmates." The process of identity and loyalty was easier to see with this artificial culture learned in an hour, creating new classroom bonds as it raised questions about the legitimacy of us and them. One American student wrote how struck he was, "not with the confusion of being an outsider to a new culture, but rather the surprising cult-like fashion of being a member of a group yourself."

The course poked holes at identity in this way by questioning the structures and boundaries dividing me from you and us from them. While the truths and satisfactions of these divisions in identity that brought meaning and belonging were acknowledged, so too were their falsities and problematic implications.

Results

In the sections that follow, I describe the outcomes of the course and the impact of the experience upon student identity.

The Boundaries of Friendship. One of the clearest and most dramatic outcomes in the course was the shift in personal social networks. I asked students on the first day of class and on the last day of class to name anyone in the class they considered a friend. Despite numerous student responses in the postquestionnaire that they were only including close friends and not acquaintances, the shift in patterns from the pre- to postresponses was fairly dramatic, as the networks in Figure 8.1 demonstrate.

Friendship ties in the class went from 99% internal to one's culture (on the first day of class) to an overall friendship network that was 50% same culture and 50% cross-cultural by the last day, as shown in Tables 8.1 and 8.2.

Moreover, U.S. students, who characteristically had no or few friendship ties at all within class, crossed the academic/personal boundary by developing several friendships with classmates, both U.S. and international, that extended beyond the classroom.

Empathy and Echoing. It can be argued that friendships connect us in more empathic ways and that empathy can shift our understanding and open our points of view. There was abundant evidence of such a shift in students' weekly journals, in their interview papers, and in their self-statements about what they learned. In the brief postquestionnaire, however, which simply asked students to name some characteristics of the three national cultures in the class, empathy was expressed in the form of "echoing," students coming to talk about the others more as the others talk about themselves.

Since I had both pre- and postdata where students said something about themselves and then said something about the two other cultures in the class, I looked to see how students' view of other cultures changed in relation to the other culture's perspective. For example, in the pretest, Chinese students frequently described their own culture with a reference to

Figure 8.1. Social Networks by Nationality on the First Day of Class and the Last Day of Class

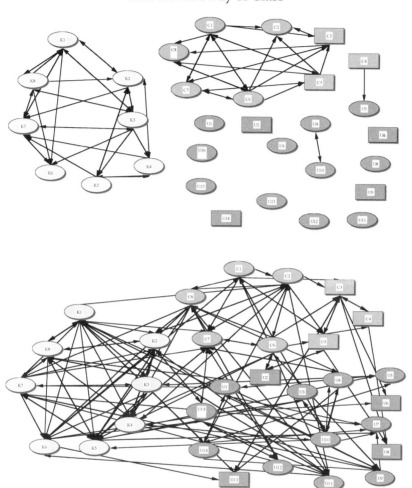

In the diagram: U = U.S. student; K = Korean student; C = Chinese student

holidays and festivals; Americans frequently used qualities of autonomy and diversity as self-referents. Would Americans and Chinese "echo" each other's self-understandings more frequently in their post statements?

Apparently, they did. There were six responses in the prequestionnaire in which Americans characterized Chinese with reference to holidays or Chinese characterized Americans as diverse or individualistic. In the postquestionnaire, there were 17 responses of this "echoing" sort, something I attribute not to my lectures or readings but to the results of student-to-student interactions both inside and outside the classroom. Students, in effect, took on the self-descriptions of their international partners.

NEW DIRECTIONS FOR HIGHER EDUCATION • DOI: 10.1002/he

Table 8.1. In-Group and Out-Group Friendship Ties on the First Day of Class

Students	In-Group Ties	Out-Group Ties	Total Ties/Ratio
Chinese	25	0	25
Korean	42	0	42
U.S.	2	1	3
Total	69	1	70 (99% internal)

Table 8.2. In-Group and Out-Group Friendship Ties on the Last Day of Class

Students	In-Group Ties	Out-Group Ties	Total Ties/Ratio
Chinese	24	26	50
Korean	39	25	64
U.S.	20	32	52
Total	83	83	166 (50% internal)

Knowledge of Self and Other.   As one might expect, knowledge of the other cultural groups in the class increased—even though course readings and lectures cast a much wider cross-cultural net than cultures represented in the class. This was expressed in pre- and postinstruments by an increase in comments and words of description about other groups. U.S. students as a group, in particular, knew little about the other cultures in the class. When asked to write five brief comments each about Korean or Chinese culture on the first day, they left two-thirds (105/160) of the comment lines completely blank. In all, their descriptions of Chinese and Korean cultures totaled 245 words. There was a significant change when the same instructions were given on the last day, when verbiage almost tripled and the number of blanks reduced to 15%. Although the change was less dramatic among Asian students, the same pattern occurred: description increased (+46%) and blanks decreased (−25%).

More surprising to me were the pre- and poststatements about one's own culture, which collectively declined in both number and words. I expected that views of self would be sharper at the end of the class and give rise to more statements with more verbiage. Given that students were *more* verbose about other cultures in the postexercise (ruling out an end-of-semester torpor affecting this not-for-credit exercise), I interpret their thinner descriptions of themselves as evidence of a self-questioning, a discomfort in asserting who they are as clearly as at the beginning of the class. In keeping with what I hoped might be an effect of the class, student identities are, perhaps, a little more fluid.

Us and Them.   In tandem with this less certain view of self was a changing sense of us and them. Talking about culture can lend itself to

Table 8.3. Number and Percent of Student Learning Reports About "One's Own Culture" vs. "Another Culture"

Learning Was About	One's Own Culture	Another Culture	% Own Culture/Total
American (U.S.)	21	15	21/36 = 58%
Asian (Chinese and Korean)	13	13	13/26 = 50%
All students	34	28	34/62 = 55%

highlighting difference—something I certainly do as an anthropologist—but this can easily lead to Black and White; either/or versions of culture and identity. Chinese are this way; Americans do this; Koreans think this way.

While students were more aware of cultural differences at the end of the class than at the beginning as boundaries of self and other shifted, students made more statements about "sameness" and their sense of group identity was more nuanced. I tried to capture this by coding pre–post statements made about one's own and other cultures for statements of "sameness" and statements of "contradiction/paradox" (e.g., this Korean student's observation: "U.S. students show much individualism but they also do a lot of volunteer and service work"). It is telling that the 12 statements of sameness or paradox that appeared in the data all occurred in the postclass comments.

Student Learning.   Although students were less inclined by the end of class to characterize their own national identities, their perception was very clearly that this class, focusing on cross-cultural information and interaction, had the effect of increasing their self-understanding. The final course assignment asked each student to identify his/her three most poignant learning outcomes during the semester. I analyzed their narratives, using Atlas Ti software, with a rubric that coded each outcome included as follows: primarily about self/one's own culture, primarily about other/another culture, or deals with other issues. A single narrative could have several codes assigned to reflect the different points addressed. A total of 62 learning outcomes were coded that mentioned knowledge of one's self or own culture or knowledge of another culture or my partner's point of view, as listed in Table 8.3.

It was interesting to see that, in student perception, learning outcomes related to self and one's own culture were slightly more prominent than those related to cross-cultural awareness. As one student expressed it, "I thought that this would be a great opportunity to learn about different cultures when I am unable to study abroad at this time. I did not really think I would end up learning about myself." These data point to the complex web in which self-understanding is situated and by inference the interactional and interpersonal nature of identity development.

In some ways, the less quantitative representations tell the story the best. I had never before taught a class where students independently set up their own Facebook page so that they could stay in touch, where every single class member showed up for an optional, nongraded, midweek dinner during the semester, where half of the class attended a "get together" at the student union a semester after the class ended, or where one "pod" of international and U.S. students invited me to join them on an out-of-town hiking outing three months after the class was over. There was simply something different happening here that speaks to the impact of peer-to-peer learning, of loosening boundaries between us and them, and of connecting an academic experience to personal and social identity.

Conclusion and Implications

U.S. universities have seen the number of international students grow eightfold since the 1960s, with an almost 50% growth in students since just 2005 (Institute of International Education, 2012). U.S. campuses have never in our history been more diverse. Our global and ethnic diversity can play a powerful role in creating a transformative educational system, where college life spurs profound inquiry into worldview and identity. To enlist this potential, however, requires more conscious structures and pedagogy than simply the shared space of campus life and classes. As educators, we need to build in the opportunities for meaningful and reflective interaction among diverse groups.

The possibilities are not limited to anthropology or social science classes. What worked about the class described in this chapter are strategies that can be fruitfully applied and adjusted for diverse subject areas. These strategies include the following:

1. *Creating crosscutting "communities" with shared goals.* In my class, "Alpha" and "Beta" cultures or arranged versus love/marriage debate teams were examples of created communities that crosscut nationality. They gave students a feeling of camaraderie across national divides. Teachers can find discipline-appropriate ways to "mix up" their classrooms, with the awareness that teacher-organized student partnerships or groups will fly in the face of the American premium on "choice"—a cultural value that can serve as the first reflexive lesson!

2. *Designing structures for intimacy and depth.* It requires activities that go beyond the classroom and attempts connections beyond the superficial. There are various ways to accomplish this besides requiring (as I did) that students meet their partners' parents and cook a meal together. In every field—from film studies to astronomy—one could devise a shared assignment related to the discipline that melds academic and social life, such as attending on- or off-campus events

together. This is a ripe area for faculty to work together with campus residence life personnel, and with "living-learning" communities or similar structures that attempt the same academic/social connections.

The key is to blur social and academic boundaries, while making the content of the intercultural interaction—and not just the task that the interaction accomplishes—a focus, too. This might mean, for instance, that student partners discuss and compare how they both viewed an out-of-class film attended together or keep a joint diary of team-building challenges and accomplishments that occurred as they built their robot for an engineering class.

3. *Encouraging and modeling reflexivity.* To learn interculturally, one must simultaneously reflect on one's own culture, and vice versa. I am always shocked to meet students whose stereotypes of other countries are simply confirmed by their overseas travel and study. It is usually a sign that they believed, rather than examined, their reactions; therefore, they learned little new about themselves or others from the interaction.

Reflexive assignments were a focus of my class, required weekly, in which students reacted to the cultural material—both in readings, films, or interactions—and then analyzed their interactions. Although weekly reflexive papers will not work for every class, students must be consistently and frequently directed to examine the assumptions or beliefs behind their reactions. In this way, cultural reactions, even problems, are transformed into insight. So the U.S. student who decries an assignment's group grade may learn instead about the force of American individualism while a Chinese student, baffled about how "rudely" U.S. students address teachers, confronts instead the way authority, age, and deference are linked and expressed in Chinese culture. In everything from classroom behavior to how one contributes on a group project to our assessment of social and environmental policy, the cultural ground on which we stand matters. As teachers, we must use these opinions, attitudes, reactions, and interactions in our classes—including our own—as fodder for a deeper understanding of ourselves and others.

Note

1. These video clips (from the 1980s and with more recent 2009 footage) accompany the books *Preschool in Three Cultures* (Tobin, Wu, & Davidson, 1989) and *Preschool in Three Cultures: Revisited* (Tobin et al., 2011).

References

Allport, G. (1954/1979). *The nature of prejudice.* New York, NY: Basic Books/Perseus Book Publishing.

Institute of International Education. (2012). *International student enrollment trends, 1949/50-2011/13. Open doors report on international educational exchange.* Retrieved from http://www.iie.org/opendoors

Nathan, R. [C. A. Small]. (2005). *My freshman year. What a professor learned by becoming a student.* Ithaca, NY: Cornell University Press.

Sunstein, B. S., & Chiseri-Strater, E. (2011). *Fieldworking: Reading and writing research* (4th ed.). Boston, MA: Bedford/St. Martin's.

Tobin, J. J., Wu, D. Y. H., & Davidson, D. H. (1989). *Preschool in three cultures.* Hartford, CT: Yale University Press.

Tobin, J., Hsueh, Y., & Karasawa, M. (2011). *Preschool in three cultures: Revisited.* Chicago, IL: University of Chicago Press.

Cathy A. Small is a professor of anthropology at Northern Arizona University.

9

This chapter briefly explores what a rite of passage is and is not, and the importance and benefits of such experiences to students, the college, and the larger society. The chapter also describes a practical set of strategies for integrating rites of passage into the campus community.

Seeing College as a Rite of Passage: What Might Be Possible

David G. Blumenkrantz, Marc B. Goldstein

College is a community of diversity. Whatever else college may be to such a diverse citizenry—students, staff, faculty, administration, and parents—it is a place where young people come of age. It is a place where intentional rites of passage can be of service to a student's identity and social development, with additional benefits for the college community as well as the larger society. While many have acknowledged this to be true (Chang, 2012; Fleischer, 2010; Olkon & Smith, 2013), few institutions have fully capitalized on the natural power of college as a place of initiation. Intentionally designed rite-of-passage experiences can powerfully impact students and the greater college environment. Below, we will briefly explore what a rite of passage is (and is not), the importance and benefits of such experiences, and some practical strategies for integrating rites of passage into the campus setting.

Rites and Wrongs of Passage

Unlike other major transitions, such as marriage and funerals, cultural and secular rituals in America do not effectively assist a child's transition to adulthood (Gavazzi & Blumenkrantz, 1993; Quinn, Newfield, & Protinsky, 1985; Roberts, 1983). The lack of clearly established rites of passage in America is partly due to the ambiguity about when one becomes an adult. Moreover, the ages at which youth receive certain adult privileges, such as the right to vote or right to drink, are rather arbitrary and are not related to any actual competencies or maturity on the part of the individuals who gain those privileges. In the absence of formal lines of demarcation between childhood and adulthood, youth experiment with

NEW DIRECTIONS FOR HIGHER EDUCATION, no. 166, Summer 2014 © 2014 Wiley Periodicals, Inc.
Published online in Wiley Online Library (wileyonlinelibrary.com) • DOI: 10.1002/he.20098

behaviors, which they perceive as adult behaviors, in their attempt to reach adulthood. Without purposeful rite-of-passage strategies that promote a positive transition toward adulthood, health-compromising behaviors, such as binge drinking (Commission on Substance Abuse at Colleges and Universities [CASA], 1994), hazing (Adams, 2010), and inappropriate sexual relations (McGolerick, 2010) are some of the ways emerging adults initiate themselves.

Indeed, the phrase *rite of passage* was endowed with specific meaning by its originator, anthropologist Arnold van Gennep—a meaning that went beyond merely a "first" or otherwise special experience for the individual. Van Gennep searched for common features across the panorama of cultural practices that exist in our species. His classic work (1909/1960), *The Rites of Passage*, identified one such commonality: the presence of community-centered rites of passage to mark important life transitions found in nearly all cultures. While the manifestations of these rites of passage vary across societies, van Gennep argued that they all contain an underlying sequence of three stages: separation, transition (liminality), and incorporation. We will discuss these briefly as they pertain to one critical life transition: emergence into adulthood within the context of college.

Separation according to van Gennep (1909/1960) referred to a change from the normal routine of daily life. Historically, in the case of youth, it was often a biological marker, that is, the onset of puberty. At this point, the message from family and community to adolescents was, in essence: "From this point on you must be on a journey to adulthood. You must leave (separate from) this place of childhood behind, separate from childish things, and move into adulthood for the health and benefit of yourself, your family, community, and nature." The transition to college, especially when a child leaves home, is clearly a stage of separation that spawns anxiety over the uncertainty of the new experience, that is, college. It is the place of "betwixt and between" (Turner, 1969) that forces change to occur.

During this transitory phase, there is considerable uncertainty and mystery; young people were in a place of liminality where social status was lost or unclear while they underwent instruction in the skills, values, and ethics needed for both individual and community survival (van Gennep, 1909/1960). This stage was marked by periods of extreme stress or "ordeals" that help to compel the adolescent to experience the full range of human emotions and potential. College clearly provides all these features; there is the uncertainty of new places, people, and expectations; the ordeal of mastering difficult cognitive material and stressful exams; and the instruction and support (academic and personal) to help the neophyte weather the transition.

One cannot remain in a place of ambiguity or confusion for long. From these emotionally charged and compelling experiences, adolescents grow, mature, and move into the third phase: incorporation (van Gennep, 1909/1960). Now they incorporate these lessons into life, and the lessons serve to guide and inform them of the community's expectation for living well and affirm them as emerging adults ready to be integrated into the healthy functioning of the local society. This third stage includes a public ritual experience (e.g., a graduation ceremony) in which the community affirms and sanctions the youth's new status.

While there may be some debate among scholars (see Lincoln, 1981) regarding the generalizability of van Gennep's tripartite structure (separation, liminality, and incorporation), there is little disagreement about the societal importance of publically sanctioned rites of passage and the implications of their absence (e.g., Blumenkrantz, 1992; Campbell & Moyers, 1988; Mahdi, Foster, & Little, 1987; Meade, 1993). Indeed, the absence of rites of passage for today's youth, families, and communities has extraordinary consequences—mostly negative—to which the above authors would attest. The rite-of-passage process not only guides the individual's transition to a new status, but, more importantly, it reaffirms and celebrates society's values. Rite-of-passage experiences are integral parts of community life. They initiate individuals into the roles and responsibilities of their new status. These public events are cause for social gathering and renewal, reinforcing the importance of these statuses, and the values accompanying them (Blumenkrantz, 1996).

The decline of communally sanctioned rite-of-passage experiences to support the transition from childhood to adulthood has spawned the growth of contemporary programs to fill this gap (Benjamin, 2011). Most such programs engage participants from a weekend to several weeks in settings *away* from one's home. While such retreats undoubtedly provide personal growth for participants and enhance bonding with their cohort, we believe that such experiences do little to foster the sense of connection, bonding, or obligation participants have to the social setting to which they return and live. Indeed, it is this absence of a place-based grounding that reflects a fundamental dilemma in many contemporary applications of rites of passage. Such programs are seen principally as an experience for the individual participant rather than for the community. Thus, rite-of-passage experiences as offered by practitioners are viewed as programs to be purchased for personal growth.

In contrast to this program orientation, we prefer a systems perspective favored by some evolutionary biologists (Wilson, 2012) who suggest that the community is the central unit of human organization. With this orientation, rites of passage were first and foremost designed to foster and strengthen the bonds of the local human ecology, insuring their resilience and adaptability, and serving the survival of our species.

Rites of Passage and Higher Education

Given the geographic mobility in contemporary society, college is a natural place for prosocial, community-sanctioned initiation, and rites of passage toward adulthood to occur. For four or more years, colleges and universities represent a diverse setting in which young people are heavily invested. Moreover, colleges generally possess more autonomy than secondary schools to shape their environments in creative ways to benefit their constituents: students, staff, faculty, and the larger society. Creating rite-of-passage experiences can be achieved through a step-by-step change process that engages multiple constituencies within the college or university. It begins by reframing college as a place of initiation, where young people come of age and upper-division students and adults are trained as *elders* and participate in the initiatory process to guide and support a student's healthy growth and development. In what follows, we present a contemporary definition of rites of passage, followed by a blueprint identifying the primary elements of an architectural structure for building rites of passage. First, a contemporary definition:

> The degree to which a series of activities are a rite of passage is directly proportional to a community's acceptance and participation in the activities and youth's perception and belief in the activities as fulfilling their conscious and unconscious needs for transformative experiences. That is, a modern day rite of passage is achieved when parents (and/or their surrogates) and the community create and participate in experiences, which are perceived to be transformative by youth and in fact offer them increased status within the community and facilitate their healthy transition through adolescence. Equally important, the celebration of a rite of passage is renewing for the entire community. A youth's public expression of and commitment to a community's values and beliefs reinforces expectations for behaviors for the entire community. A child's coming of age presents an opportunity for the whole community to examine, adapt and re-commit themselves to their social and cultural heritage. (Blumenkrantz, 1996, p. 21)

This collective involvement in creating and sustaining these essential processes is the way to strengthen the social bonds of the group. Rites of passage are rich with history and tradition that speak to our most basic human understanding, both within the unconscious and conscious mind, and as such can be effective at motivating and mobilizing a community into action on behalf of its youth. They have specific elements that when integrated through collaborative conversations can strengthen a sense of community.

College as a Place of Initiation

As noted above, college life provides experiences consistent with the phases of a rite of passage. What is missing is the lack of consistency and intentionality on the part of the college to focus these rite-of-passage experiences for the full development of their students. It is largely left up to the students to "understand" their college experience within their own development as a rite of passage and "put the pieces together." What would we be doing if we reframed college as a place of initiation?

Convening conversations around questions that matter related to welcoming everyone into the social fabric of the college campus is a first step. The conversations are intentionally guided by a series of questions that begin to uncover how rites of passage can be integrated into campus life using elements of the architectural structure for youth and community development through rites of passage as a framework (Blumenkrantz & Goldstein, 2010). The first seven elements guide an exploration into the present situation (i.e., how we welcome people to the college) and open the possibility that things may need to change. They reflect the "separation" phase of rites of passage. Below are sample questions, but the best questions come from the stakeholders within institutions:

1. *What is the story?* What is the mission and vision of our institution? In what way do mission and vision address the social, psychological, and emotional development of our members that support their own individual growth and the creation of a culture of caring and connection?

   What conditions and/or activities presently exist within the college setting that are already aligned with rites of passage (e.g., first-year experience programs, fraternities or sororities, clubs, and athletics)? Where are there access points to begin conversations about how we orient or initiate students to the values and ethics of the college or university in ways that serve to strengthen the communal bonds among everyone in the college environs?

2. *What are the values and ethics in the story?* How have values and ethics shaped our attitudes that inform and guide the decisions we make about what we do? If the institutional mission speaks of personal development and connection with the community, who is responsible for this function? Is it left up to one department—student life—or is it seriously integrated into the actions of the whole college?

3. *Is a paradigm shift necessary?* As we explore the present situation or the story that is our college's mission, how can we begin to accept the possibility that changing views—a paradigm shift—might be necessary? If we reframed the college as a place of initiation, what would we do differently? What changes might be possible, for students, staff, faculty, and administrators if this became the question that defined the college paradigm? Challenging and changing longstanding paradigms is tough work, particularly in the tradition-bound world of the academy. But it is the discussion of these fundamental questions that will let us see new possibilities and generate the energy to move toward change.

4. *Does the college foster relationships necessary for rite-of passage program success?* Where do the conditions presently exist for the formation of positive relationships that are sustained during a person's membership in our community? How are our residence halls, athletic departments, fraternities and sororities, individual disciplines/departments presently organized to build meaningful and lasting relationships that support initiating students into our college ecology?

5. *How can we make use of community "elders"?* Where might mentors, upper-class students, and "elders" naturally assist new members of the community? What can we do to intentionally prepare segments of the college to initiate incoming members in ways that strengthen bonds and create a culture of caring? How are faculty, staff, and other adults welcomed into the community that gives them a sense of connection and commitment?

6. *How can we assure that welcoming happens in the home community?* How do we define our community? Who are its members? What are their roles and responsibilities, especially as they relate to welcoming and initiating new members? Do the various subcommunities of our campus—for example, academics, student life, and administration—initiate students in ways that do not present conflicting messages or values? What is the relationship of our college with the larger community, region, nature, and the world?

7. *What are behaviors between all members of our community that exhibit respect and responsibility?* What forums within our college or university could be refocused on active deliberation and commitment to these behaviors? What programs already exist that convey values and ethics for our students in ways that deepen their commitment to both our campus and the larger community and are expressed through service?

8. *How can rites of passage create expectations for socially appropriate behaviors?* What programs already exist that convey values and ethics for our students in ways that deepen their commitment to both our campus and the larger community and are expressed through service?

Table 9.1 summarizes the early sequence of processes that colleges might work through as they transform themselves into initiatory settings.

Our preliminary efforts to initiate such changes in college settings have suggested that the biggest challenge is getting the various campus constituencies to think more broadly about their ultimate purpose. The silo mentality (Holden & Goldstein, 2010; Upton, 2010) on campuses is reinforced by an organizational structure that divides us by disciplines and obscures our recognition that we all must contribute, in a coherent way, to the full development of the next generation. Such development must go beyond intellectual prowess and incorporate the values and responsibilities needed for the successful continuity of our species. As we enter an era where

Table 9.1. Transforming College Into a Place of Initiation and Rite of Passage (ROP)[a]

Components	Element—Activities	Target Population	Outcomes
Reframing college experience as a rite of passage. Increase understanding of history, practice, and consequences of the absences of ROP.	Bring diverse constituencies together to engage in a process of discovery where conditions already exist for ROP experiences (first-year experience) and strategic planning to formulate ongoing health promotion strategies that incorporate rites of passage. Small and large group discussions, lecture, and experiences.	Administrators, key faculty, student life coordinators, resident advisors, Greek societies, sports, student services, and so forth. May include community participation in rite-of-passage experiences.	Increase understanding of rites of passage as foundation for further discussion, visioning, and development of college Rite Of Passage Experience©. Shift *frame* for college as a place of initiation.
Assess present teaching and use of rites of passage. Where do conditions already exist?	Survey campus for academic links to rites of passage within curriculum; how sports, clubs, Greek organizations, and so forth welcome and orient new members.	Faculty, Greek organizations, clubs, sports, and so forth. May also engage community at large in process of assessment if expanded rites of passage are possible.	Identification of assets in place that can support application in multiple settings of rites of passage.
What are the central values and ethics needing transmission, and how to put these into rite-of-passage strategies?	Survey students, faculty, and staff about the core values and ethics that are central to the college/university's mission. How are they presently being transmitted in ways that lead to committed behavior for the good of the individual, college, and wider community?	College community	Identify the central values and ethics of the college community. Create strategies for more potent orientation that leads to students and the entire community enacting these core values and ethics in their behaviors.

(Continued)

Table 9.1. Continued

Components	Element—Activities	Target Population	Outcomes
Build capacity for college community to become "elders" in the college rite of passage.	Training including rite-of-passage college curriculum and existing strategies such as: the Rite Of Passage Experience© (ROPE®) sessions.	Upper-class and graduate student, faculty, administrators, student services, resident life and others. May include community school representatives.	Build personnel infrastructure to support rites of passage within multiple and diverse settings within the college and community. Build mentoring system.
Trained "elders" become "leadership team" and vision how best to begin and institutionalize rites of passage across campus.	Strategic planning among leadership team and key university administration and staff. All participate in training cited above.	Upper-class and graduate students, faculty, administration, student services, resident life, and others. May include community school representatives.	Establishes strategic planning process and "leadership team," members of which become "expert" elders that guide installation of college ROPE®.
Trained "elders" begin to institute college rites of passage, such as college ROPE® at identified settings across campus.	Expansion of rites of passage college course, Rite Of Passage Experience©, and other rites of passage activities. Train mentors.	Resident advisors provide rite-of-passage experiences to students, incorporated into first-year experience.	College ROP implementation to promote health and decrease health-compromising behaviors. Deploy mentors.
Parent Rite Of Passage Experience©—ROPE®	Parent focus on "letting go well" and how parents can support their students' adjustment to and success in college.	Parents—setting to be determined by leadership team.	Parents are involved in appropriate ways to support their child. Overall increase in support of the college experience.

aFor more description of these processes see www.rope.org. The Rite of Passage Experience© and ROPE® are copyrighted (1981, 1988) and federally registered trademarks of David Blumenkrantz licensed to The Center for the Advancement of Youth, Family, and Community Services, Inc.

students and society have begun to question the value of going to college, we believe that efforts to reconceptualize college as a place of initiation and focused personal development may provide the benefits needed by students and society.

References

Adams, G. (2010, October 6). Hazing: When rites of passage go wrong. *The Independent*. Retrieved from http://www.independent.co.uk/news/world/americas/hazing-when-rites-of-passage-go-wrong-8200084.html

Benjamin, M. L. (2011). *Rites of passage programs as positive youth development* (Unpublished master's thesis). Central CT State University, New Britain, CT. Retrieved from http://content.library.ccsu.edu/cdm/singleitem/collection/ccsutheses/id/1673/rec/1

Blumenkrantz, D. (1992). *Fulfilling the promise of children's services*. San Francisco, CA: Jossey-Bass.

Blumenkrantz, D. G. (1996). The rite way: Guiding youth to adulthood and the problem of communitas. *Dissertation Abstract International*, 57(11), 4645A. (UMI No. AAT 9713085)

Blumenkrantz, D. G., & Goldstein, M. B. (2010). Rites of passage as a framework for community interventions with youth. *Global Journal of Community Psychology Practice*, 1(2), 41–50. Retrieved from http://www.gjcpp.org/pdfs/2009-0026-final-20100827.pdf

Campbell, J., & Moyers, B. (1988). *The power of myth*. New York, NY: Anchor Books.

Chang, M. (2012). College: Rite of passage. *Kaleidoscope*. Retrieved from http://studentmedia.uab.edu/2012/06/college-rite-of-passage/

Commission on Substance Abuse at Colleges and Universities (CASA). (1994). *Rethinking rites of passage: Substance abuse on America's campuses*. Retrieved from http://www.casacolumbia.org/articlefiles/379-rethinking_rites_of_passage.pdf

Fleischer, L. (2010). The journey to a genuine life: Mentoring the passage to adulthood. *Encounter: Education for meaning and social justice*, 23(2), 1–6. Retrieved from https://great-ideas.org/Encounter232/Fleischer232Print.pdf

Gavazzi, S. M., & Blumenkrantz, D. G. (1993). Facilitating clinical work with adolescents and their families through the rite of passage experience program. *Journal of Family Psychotherapy*, 4(2), 47–67.

Holden, T., & Goldstein, B. (2010, August 29). How to create a problem-solving institution. *The Chronicle of Higher Education*. Retrieved from http://chronicle.com/article/How-to-Create-a/124153

Lincoln, B. (1981). *Emerging from the chrysalis: Rituals of women's initiation*. Cambridge, MA: Harvard University Press.

Mahdi, L., Foster, S., & Little, M. (Eds.). (1987). *Betwixt and between: Patterns of masculine and feminine initiation*. LaSalle, IL: Open Court Press.

McGolerick, E. (2010). College sex: What parents need to know. *Sheknows® parenting*. Retrieved from http://www.sheknows.com/parenting/articles/817449/What-parents-need-to-know-about-college-sex

Meade, M. (1993). *Men and the water of life: Initiation and the tempering of men*. San Francisco, CA: Harper Collins.

Olkon, S., & Smith, J. (2013). *Rite of passage*. Retrieved from http://college.uchicago.edu/video/rite-passage

Quinn, W. H., Newfield, N. A., & Protinsky, H. O. (1985). Rites of passage in families with adolescents. *Family Process*, 24, 101–111.

Roberts, W. O. (1983). *Initiation to adulthood: Ancient rite of passage in contemporary form*. New York, NY: Pilgrim Press.

Turner, V. (1969). *The ritual process: Structure and anti-structure.* Chicago, IL: Aldine De Gruyter.

Upton, A. (2010, August 30). *Silo mentality and problem solving in higher education institutions* [BCD Webmasters Blog]. Retrieved from http://bcdwp.web.tamhsc.edu/webmaster/2010/08/30/

van Gennep, A. (1960). *The rites of passage* (M. B. Vizedom & G. L. Caffee, Trans.). Chicago, IL: University of Chicago Press. (Original work published in 1909)

Wilson, W. O. (2012). *The social conquest of earth.* New York, NY: W. W. Norton.

DAVID G. BLUMENKRANTZ *is the executive director of The Center for the Advancement of Youth, Family, and Community Services, Incorporated, in Glastonbury, Connecticut.*

MARC B. GOLDSTEIN *is professor emeritus of psychology at Central Connecticut State University.*

10

This chapter explains the meaning of meaning-making for the quarterlife generation. It describes what is called the meaning-quest—consisting of nine core meaning-making questions—and offers two examples of the pedagogy that the authors use in working with students.

Education for Making Meaning

Robert J. Nash, Jennifer J. J. Jang

Higher education is more than career preparation and learning how to take, and pass, exams. While both of these objectives are important, we believe that it is equally important for college students to make an enduring meaning in their lives and to learn how to pursue worthy purposes. It was Viktor Frankl (1959/2006) who said that "for the first time in human history most of us have the means to live but no meaning to live for" (p. 140). Our chapter will explain the meaning of meaning-making and will briefly describe our approach to teaching for meaning. Our teaching–learning pedagogy emphasizes the importance of storytelling and, also, what we call "moral conversation" (Nash, Bradley, & Chickering, 2008; Nash & Viray, 2013).

We base our meaning-making curriculum on what we call the "meaning-quest." This quest consists of nine core meaning-making questions that students bring to our classes each semester. Our overall objective in meaning-making teaching is to help students to integrate the self, subject matter, vocational training, moral development, religio-spiritual inclinations, and interpersonal relationships into a holistic learning experience that will prepare them for life beyond their formal education.

Why We Do What We Do as Meaning-Making Mentors

As university educators, we witness firsthand every day the need for students of all ages, both traditional and nontraditional, to have something coherent to believe in, some centering values and goals to strive for. They, like us, need strong background beliefs and ideals to shore them up during these times when religious and political wars plague entire societies; when the natural environment continues to deteriorate; and when the fluctuations of the global economy result in recession, deflation, and in the inequitable distribution of scarce resources.

New Directions for Higher Education, no. 166, Summer 2014 © 2014 Wiley Periodicals, Inc.
Published online in Wiley Online Library (wileyonlinelibrary.com) • DOI: 10.1002/he.20099

On a more personal level, the American College Health Association (2012) reports that in a sample of 76,000 students, 86% felt overwhelmed, 82% felt emotionally exhausted, 62% felt very sad, 58% felt very lonely, 52% felt enormous stress, 51% felt overwhelming anxiety, 47% felt hopeless and purposeless, and the rest felt dysfunctionally depressed. In our own teaching experience, we have found that students come to our courses on meaning-making with the need to make sense of the turmoil that results when they realize that they will graduate (if they do at all) with tens of thousands of dollars in loans to pay off; when their friendships go awry; when their work grows tedious and unsatisfying; when they become disillusioned by a sense of unfulfillment; when, on those dreaded occasions, they hear that someone they love suffers from the ravages of a metastatic malignancy; when they face life-altering decisions; or when they learn that the person who means the most to them in the whole world no longer loves them.

Education for making meaning and finding purpose holds the promise of giving a plugged-in undergraduate and graduate population permission to stop and pause in the middle of *going through the motions*. Education for making meaning enables students to talk about the deeper existential questions and universal life issues openly and honestly, and face-to-face, with significant others on campus. Meaning-making conversation forces students to take a giant step away from one of the leading addictions acknowledged worldwide (Cash, Rae, Steel, & Winkler, 2012). This includes electronic gaming, Facebook, smartphones, instant messaging, tweeting, e-mail, and all the other terminally numbing social media that control students' lives. Education for meaning-making helps students to understand the folly of living their lives obsessed with a goal-driven, get-rich-and-successful, "till then" future. Philip Larkin (quoted in Baggini, 2004) describes this condition in his poem *Next, Please*:

> Always too eager for the future, we
> Pick up bad habits of expectancy.
> Something is always approaching, every day
> *Till then*, we say . . . (p. 35)

The Meaning of Meaning-Making

> If you have your *why?* for life, then you can get along with almost any *how?*
> Frederich Nietzche (2009, p. 19)

We often spend an entire class period at the beginning of our courses digging deeply into Nietzsche's quotation above. For us, philosophy is a practical, lifelong activity that can help all of us to create "whys" for living in order to be prepared for the "hows" that so often challenge and disrupt our lives. Sharon Daloz Parks (2000) says that meaning involves the "search for a sense of connection, pattern, order, and significance . . . it is a way to understand our experience that makes sense of both the expected and un-expected . . . " (p. 10). Meaning is what sustains us during those hard, per-plexing times when everything seems to be up in the air, and there are no certain answers anywhere to the most confounding questions that plague all of us throughout our lives. Moreover, Roy Baumeister (1991) claims that all of us, without exception, strive to make sense of our lives in four basic ways: purpose, value, efficacy, and self-worth. These are the four needs for meaning—an "existential shopping list" (pp. 29–57).

We appreciate what Alan Watts (2009) said in a video-recorded inter-view about the meaning of life being a process, not a product:

> In music, one doesn't make the end of a composition the *point* of the compo-sition. If that were so, then the best conductors would be those who played the fastest! . . . People would go to a concert just to hear one crashing chord because that's the end! (0:35–1:03)

We believe that in higher education today too many students are pushed through a factory-driven education model revving up for the elu-sive and ultimate career success at the end. But, as Watts said, the end of a symphony is not the primary objective for the conductor. The focus is on the music that is being played all the way through. So, too, with meaning-making.

We believe in meaning-making as an educational dynamic that is or-ganic, interactive, and always interdisciplinary. We teach all of our courses in this way—whatever their content might be. We think of meaning-making as a process. Purpose-finding is a product, but meaning-making is fluid and evolving. Purpose-finding is more overarching and unchanging. In our meaning-making teaching, we believe in the value of tentative responses, rather than final answers, to the deepest questions and much mutual sharing of stories, passions, and beliefs. Throughout the years we have been teach-ing, we have heard our students acknowledging openly that they ceased being natural wonderers and philosophers after graduating from kinder-garten. They then proceeded to become intellectually, and emotionally, anesthetized, as they march along the educational treadmill from elemen-tary to graduate school.

In contrast, we want meaning-making to be an opportunity for all of us in higher education to grow in wisdom, especially when times get hard. We want to help our students find the paradoxes and ironies, as well as the depth, in everyday life and in the academic content they are studying. Above all, however, we want our students to *pause* throughout their col-lege experience in order to talk with empathic others about what really counts in their pursuit of a life well lived. We frequently take a planned "time-out" during our lectures, seminar conversations, group projects, mindfulness activities, or whatever else, to ask: "What is the short- and long-term meaning of what you are doing right here, right now? What do you want it to be?"

The Meaning-Making Quest for the Quarterlife Generation

Just who, and what, constitute the quarterlife generation (Robbins, 2004)? Robbins asserts that the quarterlife period (roughly between the ages of 18 and 30) is frequently a tumultuous time for most of our students, because it triggers an overwhelming anxiety about the past, present, and future. Many of our quarterlife students are plagued with worry about failure—living up to others' expectations, letting go of the comfortable securities of childhood, coming to terms with the growing tension between freedom and responsibility, and constantly comparing themselves to peers and coming up short. For so many quarterlifers, their existence seems vapid and empty.

As debilitating as is the quarterlifer's lament of meaninglessness, many quarterlifers are surprisingly articulate about the conditions that are disturbing their equilibrium. Unfortunately, however, they do not seem to recognize that these conditions are the very source of their malaise—often a result of their unrealistic expectation that someday they will be rich and famous (Pew Research Center, 2007).

Most quarterlifers we know wonder out loud why, increasingly, they experience so many of their successes as failures. We have found that, for these particular students, who tend to live their daily lives at the perfectionist, career-driven, achievement-obsessed extremes, normal fears can often lead to crushing anxiety or to debilitating depression. While medication and talk therapy can help to allay these more severe psychological symptoms, a sense of meaninglessness lingers among many quarterlifers ... often throughout their lifetimes.

In what follows, we offer a set of meaning-making questions. Each question can be thought of as a challenge that students must deal with every day. No matter a student's age, stage, vector, phase, or cycle of development, these questions get recirculated over and over again. While it is true that students of all ages experience the sets of questions differently, depending on the particular life-narrative they and we are living in at any given time, the questions still make demands on us. They are never resolved once and for all—until that magic time comes when we will live happily and challenge free ever after.

We prefer not to think of the quarterlife (or mid-life or later-life) experience as a *crisis* but rather as a series of exciting, real-life possibilities for students to make meaning. While it is true that some students do live their quarterlife years in a narrative of panic, stress, and insecurity, others live in very different narratives of meaning. Here are several big and little meaning questions that come up again and again among our quarterlifers, in our classes, in our offices, or over coffee at various times in a variety of locations, regardless of the particular narratives they might be inhabiting (see Nash & Jang, 2013):

1. *How do I realize my hopes and dreams?* What is it that I want to do with my life? How do I find the intersection between my talent and my passion? What is the balance between achievement and fulfillment?

2. *Who am I as a moral and ethical person?* Just who is it I'm striving to become as a moral being, and is this possible given all the craziness and contradictions in my life? What does it mean to live a "good life"? Aren't all values, morals, and ethics relative anyway?

3. *Can I be both religious and spiritual at the same time?* What is the right religion for me? Is there any other way to make a meaning that endures without spirituality? Will I be able to make it in the world without experiencing the consolations of organized religion along with its supportive communities?

4. *How can I construct durable, loving, and reciprocal core relationships?* Why is it so hard to live alone but also so hard to sustain a relationship? Is there really such a person as a "soulmate"? Why can't I find close, enduring friends who stay the course without drifting away? Who will be my true friends, will I ever fit in, and how will I know who I can trust?

5. *How do my and others' various identities help me to define who I am?* Who am I in relation to my skin color, social class, sexual orientation, religious background, and gender? Why can't I like who I am, whoever that might be? Why does it sometimes seem that people are so quick to put others in an identity box?

6. *How do I know that what I am studying is right for me both now and beyond college?* Is college really necessary for my future success? Why do I have to take so many required courses that don't relate to what I enjoy, aspire to, or find useful? How can I avoid the lure of "credential enslavement"?

7. *How can I transform a financially stable job/career into a soul-satisfying vocation?* Will I always have to choose between doing what I love and making lots of money? Is it possible to find a career that is congruent with my personal values? Why is it that I feel I have so much potential, but am afraid to actualize it? How will I ever be able to learn all the skills I need to be financially savvy?

8. *How can I fulfill my civic responsibility to improve the world locally, nationally, and internationally?* How do I pick my social causes, and is this even important? Is active civic engagement even possible for me given all the demands on my time both now and in the future? How will my volunteer activities enhance my resume for future endeavors?

NEW DIRECTIONS FOR HIGHER EDUCATION • DOI: 10.1002/he

9. *How can I achieve and maintain overall wellness and balance in my life?* How can I practice self-compassion when the multiple demands on my life are so intense? Is multitasking the healthiest way to live a life? Is it really possible for someone to be psychologically, physically, spiritually, emotionally, and socially healthy, all at the same time? Or are "self-care compromise" and "compassion fatigue" the realities that I will face for the rest of my life?

Our Meaning-Making Pedagogy

In the following sections, we offer a discussion of storytelling and moral conversations—key elements of meaning-making.

Storytelling.   Effective educators understand that helping students to make meaning is directly related to the ability to tell their own personal stories of meaning-making. Even better, good educators, no matter what they teach, are not afraid to evoke such personal stories from their students. Tell a story of personal meaning as you teach and advise, and you have captured your students' attention. Draw out your students' personal stories of meaning, and you have won them over for life. We appreciate the words of Sara Lawrence-Lightfoot (2000) on stories:

> Teaching is storytelling. It is the place where lives can meet . . . Stories create intimate conversations across boundaries. Stories disturb and challenge. I use stories to create deeper connections with my students, to reveal the universal human themes that we share, and to bridge the realms of thinking and feeling . . . (pp. 111–112)

We believe that stories confer survival benefits on all of us. Stories make us human. They give our lives focus. They get us up in the morning and off to work. They help us to solve problems and to survive with dignity, style, and grace. We live in our stories about what we narrate to be the "real world." For some of us, our story of life is a win–lose athletic contest. For others, life is a love affair. For others, life is a cosmic or spiritual quest. For some, life is a business venture. For others, life is one long, unmitigated catastrophe. All these stories color how we see and experience the world. However different, each of us inhabits a particular narrative at all times. And this narrative understanding affects others, just as their narratives affect us.

We try very hard to listen to our students' stories in response to some, or all, of the meaning questions above. How, for example, can we truly understand how a student will respond to a challenging reading or writing assignment, a piece of difficult advice, or a well-intentioned criticism or recommendation, without first understanding the story that a student might be living in at any given time? Why, then, not ask students to tell their stories, along with testing them for subject-matter mastery? In fact, why can't professors tell their own stories about why their disciplines are important to them?

Even better, why not teach students to *write* their way into meaning in a narrative style that incorporates, but sometimes transcends, the usual research formulas, rubrics, or templates? We call this type of writing methodology Scholarly Personal Narrative (SPN) writing (Nash, 2004; Nash & Viray, 2013). SPN writing takes personal risks. It begins with the self-confidence that the author has a personal story worth telling and a lesson worth conveying. The author's voice is personal, clear, fallible, and honest. It is a thoughtful, first-person attempt to make a point, or teach a lesson, by drawing on the author's own life experiences to provide both context and content for the course material.

Moral Conversation.   Conversation (from the Latin word, *conversare*, "to live together in order to learn about oneself and others") is an invaluable prerequisite for making meaning throughout the college years. We live in conversation with others because we enjoy it. Faculty, staff, and students enjoy it. We caress each other with the words we choose. We can also hurt each other with the words we use. We can open spaces, or we can restrict them, in our conversations both in and out of the classroom, the residence hall, and the office. We can make our learning spaces safe and comfortable, or we can make them threatening and coercive. We can spend all our time debating, pontificating, telling, critiquing, and complaining. Or we can spend much of our time in our learning spaces connecting with one another, drawing out one another, and educating—through honest give-and-take conversation—about what is inspiring in the search for meaning in the lessons and events of the day.

In our own teaching, the classroom sparkles most during those times when we are really conversing with one another. There is an honest, deeply respectful interchange about the things we agree and disagree on. In this sense, when moral conversation is working well, we are all educators. We talk together. We learn from one another. We make meaning together. It never gets tired or old. We exist in solidarity with one another, both in the classroom and in the workplace. No matter how high-pressured or technical our work, conversation is possible, even necessary.

Why do we call this type of interchange *moral* conversation? We base all our work in our meaning-making classroom on what we call the "Platinum Rule of Teaching": converse with others, as they would like to be conversed with. Moral conversation has no prior agendas—no special intellectual, philosophical, or political ideals to impose. Instead, moral conversation is a reciprocal process: it encourages us to get to know our students individually and to treat them as they would like to be treated. What we have learned through the years is that the most long-lasting education is about making meaning. But in order to start, sustain, and finish a productive conversation on meaning-making, all of us need to work together. We need to learn together. We need to learn how to enjoy one another. We stand to gain through our collaboration, because we are all equals in the effort to find, and create, a sustaining meaning in life.

Conclusion

In conclusion, one of the great pedagogical rewards for us and for our students in engaging in moral conversation and in helping one another to construct vital, authentic stories of meaning is the discovery of commonality, no matter what our surface differences might be. We are reminded again and again of a quote often attributed to the poet Terence, whose simple wisdom is profound: "Nothing human is alien to me." When our pedagogy is working well, all of us are able to come together to create meanings, both individually and collectively, personally and professionally, philosophically and spiritually. We are able to retain our individual uniquenesses while learning to become communitarians, in search of meaning and purpose.

References

American College Health Association. (2012). *Undergraduate students: Reference group executive summary.* Retrieved from http://www.acha-ncha.org/docs/ACHA-NCHA-II_UNDERGRAD_ReferenceGroup_ExecutiveSummary_Spring2012.pdf

Baggini, J. (2004). *What's it all about? Philosophy & the meaning of life.* New York, NY: Oxford University Press.

Baumeister, R. F. (1991). *Meanings of life.* New York, NY: Guilford Press.

Cash, H., Rae, C., Steel, A., & Winkler, A. (2012). Internet addiction: A brief summary of research and practice. *Current Psychiatry Review, 8*(4), 292–298.

Frankl, V. (1959/2006). *Man's search for meaning.* Boston, MA: Beacon Press.

Lawrence-Lightfoot, S. (2000). *Respect: An exploration.* New York, NY: Perseus.

Nash, R. J. (2004). *Liberating scholarly writing: The power of personal narrative.* New York, NY: Teachers College Press.

Nash, R. J., Bradley, D. L., & Chickering, A. W. (2008). *How to talk about hot topics on campus: From polarization to moral conversation.* San Francisco, CA: Jossey-Bass.

Nash, R. J., & Jang, J. J. (2013). The time has come to create meaning-making centers on college campuses. *About Campus, 4,* 2–9.

Nash, R. J., & Viray, S. (2013). *Our stories matter: Liberating the voices of marginalized students through scholarly personal narrative writing.* New York, NY: Peter Lang Publishing.

Nietzche, F. (2009). *Twilight of the idols: or how to philosophize with a hammer (reissue edition).* New York: Oxford University Press.

Parks, S. D. (2000). *Big questions, worthy dreams: Mentoring young adults in their search for meaning, purpose, and faith.* San Francisco, CA: Jossey-Bass.

Pew Research Center. (2007, January 9). *A portrait of "generation next": How young people view their lives, futures, and politics.* Retrieved from http://www.people-press.org/files/legacy-pdf/300.pdf

Robbins, A. (2004). *Conquering your quarterlife crisis: Advice from twentysomethings who have been there and survived.* New York, NY: Berkley Publishing Group.

Watts, A. (2009, September 22). *On the meaning of life.* Retrieved from http://www.youtube.com/watch?v=29atSZKbmS4

ROBERT J. NASH *is a professor in the College of Education and Social Services at the University of Vermont.*

JENNIFER J. J. JANG *is the associate director of Student Diversity Programs at Champlain College.*

INDEX

HE 163 Increasing Diversity in Doctoral Education: Implications for Theory and Practice

Karri A. Holley, Joretta Joseph

Diversity is defined as those numerous elements of difference between groups of people that play significant roles in social institutions, including (but not limited to) race and ethnicity, gender, socioeconomic class, sexual orientation, and culture. Since doctoral degree recipients go on to assume roles as faculty and educators, diversity in doctoral programs is significant. By supporting graduate diversity across the academic disciplines, universities ensure that the nation's intellectual capacities and opportunities are fully realized. The authors of this volume consider diversity broadly from multiple perspectives, from race and ethnicity to institutional type, academic discipline, and national origin. Our intent is to demonstrate how diversity operates through these venues and definitions, and our hope is to stimulate a conversation about a key aspect of American higher education.

ISBN: 978-1-1187-8358-0

HE 162 Collegiate Transfer: Navigating the New Normal

Janet L. Marling

Although students have been moving between institutions and attempting to import credit for many years, current data show that transfer is becoming an increasingly common approach to higher education. This volume is dedicated to exploring this new normal and has been written with a broad constituency in mind. It is intended to assist institutions, higher education agencies, and even state legislative bodies as they navigate the challenges of serving transfer students, a diverse, integral segment of our higher education system. Most available research has explored the two-year to four-year transfer track, and the practical examples provided here often use that framework. However, real-world transition issues are not restricted to a specific higher education sector, and readers interested in the sometimes complex processes of other transfer pathways will gain valuable insight as well.

ISBN: 978-1-1187-0102-7

HE 161 Reframing Retention Strategy for Institutional Improvement

David H. Kalsbeek

In the midst of the vast collection of work that already exists on student retention, this volume addresses the apparent difficulty in gaining traction at the institutional level in improving student retention and degree completion rates—especially at larger fouryear institutions where size, complexity, and multiplicity of structures and processes present particular challenges. This volume offers a way for institutional leaders to better focus their time, energy, and resources in their retention effort by framing the way they think about it using the 4 Ps of retention strategy: *profile, progress, process,* and *promise.* This simple framework challenges long-standing, traditional assumptions about student retention that can distract and dilute institutional efforts, and helps keep those efforts sharply and singularly focused on improving retention and degree completion outcomes.

HE 160 Codes of Conduct in Academia

John M. Braxton, Nathaniel J. Bray

Chapters of this issue of New Directions for Higher Education present tenets of codes of conduct for the presidency, academic deans, admissions officers, fund-raising professionals, faculty who teach undergraduate students, and faculty who teach graduate students. The need for such codes of conduct stems from the client-serving role of colleges and universities. Such clients include prospective donors, prospective students and their families, the individual college or university, faculty members, undergraduate and graduate students, and the knowledge base of the various academic disciplines. Because presidents, academic deans, admissions officers, fund-raising professionals, and faculty members experience role ambiguity and substantial autonomy in the performance of their roles, codes of conduct are needed to protect the welfare of the clients served. The authors offer recommendations for policy and practice regarding the proposed codes of conduct. Organizational constraints and possibilities of enacting such codes are also discussed.
ISBN: 978-1-1185-3775-6

HE 159 In Transition: Adult Higher Education Governance in Private Institutions

J. Richard Ellis, Stephen D. Holtrop

Adult degree programs can pose challenges to traditional campus structures. This volume of case studies shows a number of small, independent universities addressing various administrative and service functions for their adult programs. Institutions have unique internal structures and distinctive histories, which mean some adult programs remain very connected to the central campus administrative and service functions while others develop autonomy in a number of areas. As an adult program grows, its relationship with the traditional program changes, while outside forces and internal reevaluation of priorities and finances also work to realign the balance of centralized and autonomous functions. Balancing these functions in an institution-specific hybrid structure can provide both a measure of autonomy and centralized efficiency and consistency. In the end, each institution needs to find its own balance of centralized and decentralized services and administrative functions. Mutual appreciation and collaboration are keys to finding such an institutional balance.
ISBN: 978-1-1184-7749-6

NEW DIRECTIONS FOR HIGHER EDUCATION

ORDER FORM SUBSCRIPTION AND SINGLE ISSUES

DISCOUNTED BACK ISSUES:

Use this form to receive 20% off all back issues of *New Directions for Higher Education*.
All single issues priced at **$23.20** (normally $29.00)

TITLE	ISSUE NO.	ISBN
_____	_____	_____
_____	_____	_____
_____	_____	_____

Call 888-378-2537 or see mailing instructions below. When calling, mention the promotional code JBNND to receive your discount. For a complete list of issues, please visit www.josseybass.com/go/ndhe

SUBSCRIPTIONS: (1 YEAR, 4 ISSUES)

☐ New Order ☐ Renewal

U.S.	☐ Individual: $89	☐ Institutional: $311
CANADA/MEXICO	☐ Individual: $89	☐ Institutional: $351
ALL OTHERS	☐ Individual: $113	☐ Institutional: $385

Call 888-378-2537 or see mailing and pricing instructions below.
Online subscriptions are available at www.onlinelibrary.wiley.com

ORDER TOTALS:

Issue / Subscription Amount: $ _____

Shipping Amount: $ _____
(for single issues only – subscription prices include shipping)

Total Amount: $ _____

SHIPPING CHARGES:

First Item	$6.00
Each Add'l Item	$2.00

(No sales tax for U.S. subscriptions. Canadian residents, add GST for subscription orders. Individual rate subscriptions must be paid by personal check or credit card. Individual rate subscriptions may not be resold as library copies.)

BILLING & SHIPPING INFORMATION:

☐ **PAYMENT ENCLOSED:** *(U.S. check or money order only. All payments must be in U.S. dollars.)*

☐ **CREDIT CARD:** ☐ VISA ☐ MC ☐ AMEX

Card number _____ Exp. Date _____

Card Holder Name_____ Card Issue # _____

Signature _____ Day Phone _____

☐ **BILL ME:** *(U.S. institutional orders only. Purchase order required.)*

Purchase order # _____
Federal Tax ID 13559302 • GST 89102-8052

Name _____

Address_____

Phone_____ E-mail_____

Copy or detach page and send to: **John Wiley & Sons, One Montgomery Street, Suite 1200, San Francisco, CA 94104-4594**

Order Form can also be faxed to: **888-481-2665**

PROMO JBNND

Great Resources for Higher Education Professionals

Student Affairs Today

12 issues for $225 (print) / $180 (e)

Get innovative best practices for student affairs plus lawsuit summaries to keep your institution out of legal trouble. It's packed with advice on offering effective services, assessing and funding programs, and meeting legal requirements.

studentaffairstodaynewsletter.com

Campus Legal Advisor

12 issues for $210 (print) / $170 (e)

From complying with the ADA and keeping residence halls safe to protecting the privacy of student information, this monthly publication delivers proven strategies to address the tough legal issues you face on campus.

campuslegaladvisor.com

Campus Security Report

12 issues for $210 (print) / $170 (e)

A publication that helps you effectively manage the challenges in keeping your campus, students, and employees safe. From protecting students on campus after dark to interpreting the latest laws and regulations, *Campus Security Report* has answers you need.

campussecurityreport.com

National Teaching & Learning Forum

6 issues for $65 (print or e)

From big concepts to practical details and from cutting-edge techniques to established wisdom, NTLF is your resource for cross-disciplinary discourse on student learning. With it, you'll gain insights into learning theory, classroom management, lesson planning, scholarly publishing, team teaching, online learning, pedagogical innovation, technology, and more.

ntlf.com

Disability Compliance for Higher Education

12 issues for $230 (print) / $185 (e)

This publication combines interpretation of disability laws with practical implementation strategies to help you accommodate students and staff with disabilities. It offers data collection strategies, intervention models for difficult students, service review techniques, and more.

disabilitycomplianceforhighereducation.com

Dean & Provost

12 issues for $225 (print) / $180 (e)

From budgeting to faculty tenure and from distance learning to labor relations, *Dean & Provost* gives you innovative ways to manage the challenges of leading your institution. Learn how to best use limited resources, safeguard your institution from frivolous lawsuits, and more.

deanandprovost.com

Enrollment Management Report

12 issues for $230 (print) / $185 (e)

Find out which enrollment strategies are working for your colleagues, which aren't, and why. This publication gives you practical guidance on all aspects—including records, registration, recruitment, orientation, admissions, retention, and more.

enrollmentmanagementreport.com

WANT TO SUBSCRIBE?

Go online or call: 888.378.2537.

JB JOSSEY-BASS™
A Wiley Brand